MORGAN
at LE MANS

MORGAN
at LE MANS

David Dowse

TEMPUS

This book is dedicated to Christopher Lawrence, to my wonderful sons Daniel and Henry… and to free spirits everywhere.

First published 2005

Tempus Publishing Limited
The Mill, Brimscombe Port,
Stroud, Gloucestershire, GL5 2QG
www.tempus-publishing.com

© David Dowse, 2005

The right of David Dowse to be identified as the Author
of this work has been asserted in accordance with the
Copyrights, Designs and Patents Act 1988.

All rights reserved. No part of this book may be reprinted
or reproduced or utilised in any form or by any electronic,
mechanical or other means, now known or hereafter invented,
including photocopying and recording, or in any information
storage or retrieval system, without the permission in writing
from the Publishers.

British Library Cataloguing in Publication Data.
A catalogue record for this book is available from the British Library.

ISBN 0 7524 3488 8
Typesetting and origination by Tempus Publishing Limited
Printed in Great Britain

Contents

	Introduction	7
	Prologue	8
	PART ONE - Unfinished Business	
one	A car is born	11
two	Bump starts and civil war	15
three	Testing times	21
four	The long and winding road	27
	PART TWO - On A Mission	
five	'We're going to need some sponsorship'	43
six	'Sorry about the roof, mate!'	49
seven	The Morgan Way	55
eight	Paperwork	59
nine	A star in the car	71
ten	Phoenix Rising	89
eleven	Licence to kill	95
twelve	Back on track	103
thirteen	Diversion down under	111
fourteen	Home of the Brave	121
fifteen	Testing times II	141
sixteen	Breakdown	153
seventeen	The last mile	171
	Epilogue	189
	The Morgan Works Le Mans 2004 Team	191

Introduction

This is not a story about cars or motor racing. It is a story about passionate human endeavour.

At four in the afternoon on Sunday 13 June 2004, a Morgan Aero 8 crossed the finishing line at the Le Mans 24 Hour race. It was the first car from the famous British independent marque to do so for forty-two years.

Working with a budget smaller than the catering spend of some of their competitors, borrowed equipment and large amounts of true British grit and determination, the underdogs of international motor racing had taken on the world's toughest race and won. Not the race, but the moment. It was the culmination of a two-year campaign that had seen serial shattering blows and apparently insurmountable difficulties.

The Morgan Works Team had proved to a cynical world that simply taking part still matters. Their determination, guts, good humour, skill and grace under the most extreme pressure won the hearts of the massive crowd and a world-wide TV audience – and the race authority's prize for the best crew.

Pain, frustration, politics, mistakes and corruption are all here. So are some of the remarkable characters who made it all happen and the uplifting joy of overcoming adversity. I have searched myself to answer a question that many friends have asked and that the reader may also pose as the story unfolds: why did I take on the seemingly impossible task of taking Morgan back to Le Mans?

Certainly not for financial reward; there was none – in fact, the very opposite is true. For personal glory, then? I hope not and I really don't believe so. The truth is a combination of factors. Certainly, I was touched by something very special in 2002; unfinished business that cried out, begged to be completed. The project seemed almost to choose me. Certainly, there didn't seem to be anyone else around who could or would take on the mission. I had already come to love Morgan and what it had represented for almost 100 years. And yes, maybe there quietly in the background was a small, skinny boy, desperately wanting to prove to his long-dead father that he was a child who had a lot to offer…

This book – and indeed the whole odyssey – would simply not have been possible without the kindness and faith of many individuals. Some of them are mentioned in the narrative, but it would be impossible to include everyone. They know who they are.

I hope I will be forgiven for any errors of memory or omission.

On a personal level, I must sincerely thank my good friend Steven Henson for enduring encouragement and guidance, Georgina and the boys for putting up with it all and Mr Poulton, the wonderful teacher who first inspired a little boy to read and write.

David Douse

Prologue

The longest journey starts with a single step. There were many steps along this particular journey, many of them faltering and some leading up dark, blind alleys. The history of Morgan and the heroic deeds that have been associated with the name since the earliest, pioneering days, stretches back to 1909. Readers with a historical interest will enjoy Brian Laban's excellent and authoritative book, *The first and last of the real sports cars*. But for this particular story, we have to start somewhere and as what follows concerns the true story of Morgan at Le Mans, it's most appropriate to start in 1962.

Those were very different days. At the time, I was a skinny seven-year-old. My horizon ended at the sea front in Southsea, where I would skim stones and gaze wonderingly at the exotic, mist-shrouded shores of the Isle of Wight – an alien world. I was blissfully unaware of the existence, further across the water, of France and the world's most gruelling motor race.

Many laps ahead of me in life's short race, Christopher Lawrence was then still in his twenties and he already knew all about Le Mans. His remarkable personal story is detailed elsewhere and I won't presume to retell it in detail here. Suffice to say that it was Christopher's 'devil may care' attitude that helped drive the little green Morgan Plus 4 to a famous win in the 2-litre class – and an almost equally famous drive back to England in the same car. In doing so he lit a fuse that would fizzle and pop for decades, finally to re-ignite exactly forty years later. This is the story of what happened next.

Christopher Lawrence wins the 2-litre class at Le Mans in 1962.

PART ONE

Unfinished Business

one

A car is born

The years following Christopher Lawrence's 1962 victory saw the sudden and total disappearance of the Morgan marque from top flight international motor racing. In Stuttgart, the clinical engineers at Porsche set their formidable skills to developing a racing car that would eventually evolve into a world beater.

Meanwhile, over in sleepy Malvern, the craft-based Morgan factory knew it had a winning formula already – with loyal customers all over the world who wanted anything but change. Rapid advances in chassis technology quickly overtook the British marque and though the Plus 8, launched in 1968, became an iconic sports car on the road, it could no longer provide the platform for an internationally competitive racing car. Racing Morgan owners instead happily thrived in the club racing world.

Some thirty-five years had passed since the Le Mans victory. Christopher Lawrence was now employed by Morgan as Chief Development Engineer and worked closely with Charles Morgan on the development of the radically new Morgan Aero 8 – the first completely new Morgan for sixty years. With his roots firmly planted in motor racing, it was a natural move to take the prototype Aero 8 racing.

'Big Blue', as the car became affectionately known, was a GT race car built on an early version of the Aero 8's radical aluminium chassis and dressed with modified body panels from the Plus 8 production line. Run by a small team from the factory, Big Blue raced in the 1996/97 FIA GT series in Europe. Aerodynamically challenged, it was not able to break into the pace of the Porsche and Ferrari competition, but the project delivered valuable development knowledge and, crucially, led directly to a unique relationship with BMW.

Following a chance conversation between Charles Morgan and senior BMW staff in the paddock, BMW engineers were soon visiting the Malvern factory and were immediately charmed by the Morgan magic. A more different environment from the regimented and fiercely efficient engineering regime of their Munich home could not be imagined. The Germans loved the organic way that development progressed at Morgan and in particular they liked its size and the virtually flat management structure. Instead of formal meetings, the small development team was more likely to discuss a problem over an impromptu cup of tea with Charles and Christopher. With the fantastic resource of the Morgan craftsmen on tap, ideas could quickly be tried out. The BMW and Morgan development engineers had the unique opportunity of seeing a project through all its stages and remaining 'hands on' throughout. They were like children at Christmas.

Work on the new road car continued for the next few years, resulting in the superb marriage of the Aero 8's light aluminium chassis and body panelling with the 4.4 litre BMW V8 engine, its electronic control systems specially mapped to the new car by experts at Bosch.

I joined Morgan as a PR consultant in May 2000, a few months after the company had caused a sensation by launching, at the Geneva Motor Show, the aluminium-intensive Aero 8. The first entirely new Morgan car for over sixty years, it was a very controversial development that split first the worldwide Morgan community and next the world's influential motoring media.

Why the split? There were die-hard Morgan traditionalists, both among Morgan owners around the world and also deep within the factory itself, for whom any departure from the car they knew and loved verged on the sacrilegious. In motoring circles outside the Morgan community the Aero 8's unique styling was either loved or loathed. There were few people sitting on the fence.

'The car certainly has superb technology, but what about those weird, cross-eyed headlights?' one journalist asked Charles Morgan in an early interview. Charles was very sensitive to the smallest criticism of his new car and I held my breath while he paused for a brief moment before answering:

'Well, look at it this way; if I ever make a car that people don't argue about, I will probably stop making cars and do something else.'

Charles was always a superb performer in media interviews and he was one of the very best people I have ever worked with in front of TV cameras. No doubt this was a useful legacy of his time as a news cameraman before he joined the family company.

Reporting to Charles himself and Morgan's ever cheerful sales and marketing director, Matthew Parkin, my brief was to support the launch of the new car and help deal with the implications and complications its advent generated among the fiercely conservative Morgan world. It was a fantastic opportunity to work with one of the world's most well-loved brands. Aided and abetted by my equally enthusiastic colleagues, I plunged head-first into the challenge.

The launch of the Aero had already generated a huge amount of interest in the media; and not just in Britain. We immediately had our work cut out dealing with a constant round of journalists from the world over wanting to drive the car, visit the factory, interview Charles, make TV documentaries…

Before very long my long-suffering and superbly efficient colleague Natasha Waddington and I were both completely and irrevocably immersed in the magic of Morgan. It was said even then that if you cut either of us, you would find the word Morgan running through our bones like a stick of seaside rock.

Having launched the Aero 8 road car, Christopher Lawrence was not one for sitting around idly twiddling his thumbs. In a dark, disused shed at the back of the Morgan factory, he beavered away like a contemporary Merlin with a couple of assistants to produce his next baby – the Aero 8 GTN race car.

His ultimate dream was unfolding – somehow he would take a Morgan back to Le Mans before he hung up his spanners for good. The technical challenges were considerable. Charles was very keen that the race car would conform to the FIA GTN regulations, while Christopher's Le Mans ambitions demanded that the finished car should meet with the slightly different requirements of the powerful French Automobile Club de l'Ouest (ACO) authorities.

The car that appeared publicly for the first time in January 2002 at the Autosport International Exhibition at the National Exhibition Centre in Birmingham was necessarily something of a technical compromise – it almost met both international standards, but fell a little short of meeting either one completely. There was still a lot of work to be done.

The stunning Morgan, in its Racing Green livery, attracted a lot of attention and on the first day of the show a serious customer quickly appeared. Richard Stanton, a well-known privateer on the British GT racing scene, met Christopher on the stand and they talked long and hard about one subject – Le Mans. Christopher quickly persuaded Richard that the car could and would meet all the ACO technical standards and more, that the ACO would warmly welcome an entry with this car.

Le Mans is an invitation race that is always oversubscribed. At that time, the entry process was steeped in mystery. A team with Le Mans ambitions must first apply for an invitation and then wait for the outcome of a highly secretive committee meeting. The criteria on which their decisions were made were not published in any detail. The fact that Christopher had been a previous winner and had top level personal contacts inside the ACO might therefore be a critical factor. Richard Stanton was bowled over. His long and close association with TVR – another famous British independent marque – was put aside and he plunged enthusiastically into the new project. A deposit cheque for the car was soon in the bank.

two

Bump starts and civil war

Back at the factory in the cold light of Monday morning, the news came as something of a shock. The race car was completely undeveloped – in fact when Richard bought it, it had never turned a wheel. I advised Charles that Morgan Motor Company now had a difficult and important decision to take. Morgan's return to Le Mans on the fortieth anniversary of the 1962 win, even under a private team flag, was sure to be seen by the motorsport world as a big story. And it was sure to be the famous name of Morgan that would resonate.

Essentially, the choice was quite simple; Morgan could either distance itself completely from the Le Mans entry, or it could take an active part in it and reap the rewards of the publicity storm that would surely follow.

I first met Richard Stanton soon after the decision had been taken. I travelled to an address near Winchester, where I was warmly welcomed by Richard in a beautiful and very luxurious new house. It sat in several acres of expensive rolling Hampshire countryside and a quick glance at the stable blocks, the private cinema, swimming pool and tennis courts gave an undeniable impression of considerable wealth. Richard produced coffee and toast from the huge kitchen and we discussed the outline of the Le Mans project. The major subject under consideration was the handling of DeWalt, a major sponsor that was closely tied to Richard and what I called 'the Morgan effect'. At one point, Richard phoned a colleague about the production of some graphics materials. I was party to only one side of the conversation, but one particular line, delivered in Richard's silky, seductive voice, has echoed in my mind ever since – it should be the epitaph of motorsport.

'Of course you'll get paid, Brian.'

Time was very short. Rapid arrangements were made for a media launch of the car at the Rockingham circuit. I was in constant touch with Richard as he worked at an impressive pace to ensure that team clothing, pit decoration, a big race truck and the car itself looked good for the all-important photographs. My role was to produce detailed press information and make preparations for the PR campaign that would follow the launch.

The Aero 8 GTN lines up with Aero 8 road cars at Rockingham. (Morgan Motor Company)

Opposite: Richard Stanton (left) and Steve Hyde pose with the car at Rockingham. (Morgan Motor Company)

Everyone duly turned up at Rockingham on a freezing February morning, with a piercing wind blowing straight from the Artic circle. It was a bad omen.

The car was unloaded and presented in its new black and yellow DeWalt livery. I thought it looked ugly in the garish colours, but was consoled by the thought that it would stand out well on camera. The technical team was all over, under and inside the car, preparing for its first firing up. Finally it was ready. Richard Stanton sat in the cockpit, resplendent in his new DeWalt/Morgan race suit and helmet. The cameras flashed. But the engine didn't. Even to my non-technical ear, something was obviously not right.

There followed a sad and depressing episode as the technical team, a loose affiliation of a couple of Morgan people and others from Richard's TVR camp, tried desperately to get the engine running. Batteries were soon flat and the team and invited guests were treated to the ignominious sight of a world-class Morgan race car being towed around the paddock in a vain attempt to bump start its £70,000 race engine.

I watched for a while and then retreated to the pit garage to look after a TV interview we had arranged for Charles. Thankfully, attention was quickly diverted away from the technical teething problems.

Somehow, the engine problems were temporarily sorted out and the car eventually rattled around the circuit a couple of times – long enough for the TV crew and photographers to get what they needed.

We were all issued our team clothing – a minor feeding frenzy ensuing in the freezing garage as everyone rushed to put on the welcome extra layers. The team lined up in front of the newly painted DeWalt race truck for a picture and managed a creditable smile considering the weather conditions and the inglorious start to the DeWalt/Morgan 2002 Le Mans campaign.

Back at our office, it was soon clear that the launch day had not been such a disaster, at least in PR terms. We had good pictures, some very positive TV coverage and our launch press release had achieved widespread coverage in the world's media. Mercifully, nobody seemed to have picked up on the terrible engine problems. The initial results were good for Morgan, good for DeWalt and good for Stanton. In the dingy race workshop at Malvern, though, all was far from well, despite the welcome news from France that the race invitation had indeed been confirmed by the authorities in France.

The initial skirmish I had witnessed at Rockingham between technicians from Morgan and Stanton's TVR outfit were the opening shots in a war of attrition that was to continue throughout the whole 2002 Le Mans campaign. It boiled down to a clash of personal and engineering chemistry between Christopher and Stanton's chief engineer, Dennis Leech. Both men were strong characters; stubborn and opinionated. Each held the other's view about anything in spectacularly low regard. It was not a strong foundation for a successful team and the clash at the top of the technical tree naturally trickled down to the mechanics working under them.

It was a strange dichotomy. In the blue corner stood the Morgan people, who loved the car and everything about it simply because it was a Morgan. In the red corner were the TVR men, who hated the car and everything about it simply because it was a Morgan. The Morgan crew's case was not strengthened during early testing. Time was ticking away and the car was rolled out at several British circuits in a desperate attempt to get it up to pace. The Mader-tuned BMW engine continued to give cause for serious concern and consecutive engine failures curtailed vital testing time on the track, so that handling issues could not be properly ironed out. The pressure was intense. And the blame war raged.

Dennis had strong views about the Morgan's handling and the disagreement quickly escalated into hand-to-hand combat with Christopher. Christopher was convinced that Dennis simply did not understand his unique suspension design, while Dennis was adamant that the car needed anti-roll bars. In the end, anti-roll bars were fitted. Improved performance was immediately claimed by the red corner. The blue corner quietly disconnected the roll bars without telling the drivers. The red corner did not notice any difference in handling. Lap times were disappointing, with or without the troublesome piece of metal. I was beginning to learn a little about motor racing.

Teams invited to compete in the race are required to attend a test weekend at the Le Mans circuit in April. This is designed to allow the teams to acclimatise to the conditions in which they will have to work at the big race and the drivers to get accustomed to the awesome 13.6km circuit. It also brings a few million extra Euros into the local economy and provides a useful PR platform for the ACO to promote the race itself.

In a rare example of international motorsport glamour, Natasha and I flew into Le Mans in a small private plane, courtesy of Westover, a Morgan dealer and one of the sponsors of the DeWalt team. We took off from Bournemouth and landed on the little airfield right next to the circuit, to be met by a team minibus. At the time, I don't recall either of us feeling at all important or special. In hindsight, perhaps we should have savoured our moment of VIP glory; it was not to be repeated.

Arriving for the first time in the paddock of the world's most famous race circuit is a truly memorable experience. The unique atmosphere of the place, with its decades of history, hit me the moment I stepped out into the empty, silent pit lane. Looking up at the vast grandstands, all empty now, I could almost hear the cheers of the vast crowds that had witnessed so much gladiatorial action over the years. Being a self-confessed non-motorsport person, I was surprised at the strength of my feelings as I stood there.

Finding the bright yellow DeWalt race truck among the line up of some fifty others was a simple matter even in the failing light and we found the camp in reasonably good spirits. Everyone was no doubt excited by the same unique Le Mans magic I had felt on arrival.

We found our way around the paddock, locating the vast media centre, the bars and the toilets and spent a little time with the team. There was a lot of work going on with the car, which seemed to be forever being built, dismantled and rebuilt. The first run on the track was scheduled for the following day and everyone was nervous about how the virtually untried Aero 8 would do among the field of the 'big boys'.

At the test weekend, there is an important qualifying criteria; each of the three named drivers must complete a minimum of ten laps of the circuit. Failure to do so automatically disqualifies a driver. And while there is no specific minimum lap time demanded at this stage, the ACO has *carte blanche* to banish any car which is clearly not up to scratch in performance terms. A lot of money, fragile egos and reputations were on the line. The pressure was on.

I walked slowly along the brightly lit pit lane, looking carefully at the many Porsche and Ferrari teams that were our class competitors. They all seemed worryingly calm. Not for them the burning of midnight oil just to ensure the car would start up the next day. Their superior budgets and carefully planned test programmes had ensured that their teams were either already tucked up in their hotel rooms grabbing much needed rest, or more likely were supping cold beers and talking endlessly about cars in one of the town's welcoming bars.

I tried to look with professional PR eyes and was pleased to note that Richard Stanton and his backers had done a good job in the important presentation areas. From the audience and TV camera perspective, at least, the DeWalt/Morgan camp looked every inch a professional operation.

Back at the DeWalt/Morgan camp, I talked with as many people as I could, from the most senior management to the lowly tyre cleaners and volunteer gofers, in order to get a deeper feel for what was really going on. It was not a pretty picture. Civil war was raging in the camp, aggravated by the foreign environment and the pressure to perform on the big stage. Power ebbed and flowed between the two sides. Who was really in control? The answer varied according to a complex biorhythm that involved both technical and personal chemistry. I could not fathom it. But mercifully, my job was less complex – I just had to convince the world that everything was fine and dandy. Morgan was back at Le Mans.

three

Testing times

The test weekend is open to the public just like the big race itself – although the whole event is at a much smaller level. But still, we were all amazed at the number of people who crowded around the front of the DeWalt/Morgan garage during the public pit walk sessions. Many of them were Morgan fans who had travelled there just to see the Aero 8 in action. Natasha and I spent a lot of time out front talking to them and we both became hoarse after a few hours. One memorable couple had travelled all the way from East Anglia just to have a photo taken of their little mascot teddy bear – complete with Morgan-style flying jacket and goggles – with the Aero 8. We made a fuss of them and they went away delighted that we had allowed them into the holy ground of the pit garage.

I was learning all the time. It struck me just how much impact could be made by a team that made a real effort to be open with the fans. So many other teams were aloof and closed, treating the punters as annoyances. To me, they were the *raison d'etre* of the whole crazy circus. It was so easy to make someone's day with a smile and a small gesture and it felt good to be able to hand out so much pleasure. But finally, playtime for punters was over. The pit lane was cleared very efficiently by two officials who simply walked the length of the lit lane holding a long rope between them and blowing whistles, literally herding the fans out like so many sheep. Suddenly the pit lane was clear of all except the teams. It was time for some action.

The technical team worked on the car right up to the very second before the pit lane exit lights turned green to signal the opening of the track. It was a free practice session, but run under all the strict regulations that apply during the race itself. For Morgan lovers inside and outside the pit garage, the sight of a Morgan running on the track at Le Mans was an emotional moment and Natasha and I worked quickly to get out a press release and a photograph to mark the historic milestone.

'It's no rocket machine, is it?' Driver Steve Hyde sneered as he finished his first session in the car.

The lack of proper development time was now making itself felt and the Aero 8 was circulating at a lap time of around 4 minutes 30 seconds, placing it firmly at the back of the GT field – a full 20 seconds off the pace of the class leaders.

As nervous as a proud parent at a school sports day, Christopher looked a little crestfallen, but quickly recovered his composure.

'The test is about completing ten laps each, not how fast we go,' he reminded the sceptical red corner of the team. Dennis Leech grunted an indistinguishable reply.

Money. Motorsport vaporises it faster than it does high octane fuel. The Le Mans race is estimated to bring over 200 million Euros into the local economy every year and this is just the cash spent by teams and fans on hotels, food and drinks. In order to get there, an average team in the GT class may spend several millions even before they travel to France. The spend of the top teams, like Audi, is measured in many tens of millions.

It was rumoured that the DeWalt-funded Morgan Team had something in the region of £650,000 available, but this is not a figure that any official is likely to confirm or deny. One thing I have learned about motorsport during my brief dalliance is that every financial deal associated with it is a can of worms best left unopened. What was abundantly clear from a look around the test weekend paddock was the difference between the relatively rich and the patently poor. The wealthy teams, with their immaculate state-of-the-art equipment and tools, their racks of perfectly prepared spares covering every conceivable eventuality, their *cordon bleu* catering camps and their air conditioned, soundproofed rest pods for the drivers, contrasted dramatically with the Morgan camp.

Being next-door neighbours to Audi, arguably the wealthiest team in the paddock, provided a perfect visual demonstration of the disparity. Glance to the right and you saw a set up that would not have disgraced NASA; banks of high-technology operated by highly trained specialist operators. Look left and there's the Morgan camp. A couple of notebook PCs, a few battered tool boxes and most important of all, a barbeque operated by a highly trained specialist named Billy the truckie. Billy made the best bacon sandwiches known to motorsport and so made the Morgan camp a popular stop off for the British journalists.

We made the best of it. Our line to the media was that here was a living example of the true spirit of Le Mans; a racing team that made up for what it lacked in funding with large amounts of passion and guts. A team that was 'having a go' against all the odds. The media loved it.

'*C'est le courage!*' grinned one incredulous French reporter as he left the Morgan camp.

In the press room, Natasha and I worked hard to persuade the journalists to look at us kindly.

'You already know who's going to come first, second and third', I told one of them.

'There's not much of a story in that.'

Over a glass of wine in a rare moment of quiet, I pondered on all the money that was being burned all around me. Somewhere inside a voice was asking penetrating moral questions; How can this be justified? What about the good all that money could do in poor places of the world? But at the same time I could see that the 'Spirit of Le Mans' was really all about human endeavour. In a way it represents a modern version of the gladiator stadium. And it's an outlet for international machismo and engineering capability that does not involve weapons of destruction.

My thoughts meandered further down this winding avenue. How striking it was that every year around 100,000 British fans travel to this remote venue in France, party hard and long for up to a week, generally watch their national teams easily beaten by those from foreign countries and yet create virtually no trouble and mostly leave a warm feeling with the good people of Le Mans and the other 100,000 or so non-British spectators. Think about the terrible damage a few flag-draped louts can do when they visit another country in so called 'support' for their national football team. Yes, there is something very special about Le Mans.

The main core of the team was staying in a very old chateau about 30 minutes drive away from the circuit. It sounds very glamorous. The reality was different. Although certainly very beautiful and architecturally interesting, it was dark and damp and critically for the race team, it had no bar.

As the PR team, Natasha and myself were seen as peripheral, not really part of the team; after all, we wore a distinctively Morgan flag. We were billeted instead in a cheap, rough and ready apartment hotel close to the main railway station in the city centre. The contrast from landing in the afternoon by private plane to closing the door very late the same night in a bare, soulless and plastic cheap hotel room was a poignant one. It had been a very long and eventful day. I fell on to the uncomfortable single bed and slept like a baby.

The weekend sessions saw further tense times on the track. Nobody was confident of the reliability of the engine and it was vital that all three drivers achieved their ten laps each of the long circuit. Somehow the technical team nursed it along and by the end of the first session on Sunday, we had safely booked our place at the qualifying stages during race week in June. Then it would get serious. Lap times would become the vital issue; if the Morgan was to make the starting grid, it would have to meet two further rules – a certain percentage of the lap time of the leader its class and of the average of the three fastest cars in qualifying. We were a very long way off those targets as the team started the long job of packing up and Natasha and I went off to catch a bumpy and cold ride home in the small plane that had brought us to Le Mans.

The PR continued to go very well. Boosted by photographs of the Morgan on track at Le Mans, the qualification of the drivers and the success of the 'Spirit of Le Mans' storyline, we were achieving blanket coverage. Expectations were building.

But like a swan, we were all serenity on the topside, but paddling like crazy underneath just to keep up with the current. The technical arguments escalated as everyone tried to find a way to unlock the extra performance that was clearly required in June – just a few weeks away. Christopher spent a great deal of time talking on the phone to Mader in Switzerland and BMW in Germany in an effort to solve the reliability issues and hopefully coax more horsepower from the V8 engine.

Relations between Christopher and Richard Stanton had deteriorated badly. Richard was clearly disappointed with the car's performance, but was not prepared to pay for any development work . Christopher pointed out that the car was sold 'as seen' and that all the extra work had been carried out, at Morgan's cost as agreed, to ensure that the car met all the ACO's stringent technical requirements. The entry, as promised, had materialised. The car's engine and drivetrain were not the only areas running too hot.

It was decided that a few days of final testing were essential and a plan was laid to take the car and a small support team to Miramas, BMW's superb test facility in the south of France. This was a good arrangement logistically – the team could proceed north from Miramas direct to Le Mans to arrive in good time to meet the rest of the team and set up for the big race, a week prior to race day.

It was a frantic time for the PR operation, too. We were busy with TV and radio interviews, pre-race press releases and preparing 3,000 press information packs in three languages. Plans were also made to realise an inspired idea originating from Matthew Parkin at the Morgan factory. We already worked closely with Matthew providing content and updates for the popular Morgan web site and Matthew came up with a gem – could we broadcast the action from a web cam from inside the Morgan pit garage during the race? Our colleagues and good friends at Sure Communications, the technical wizards behind the running of the web site, were enthused by the idea and assured us that there were no major technical hurdles that could not be overcome in time.

We were all excited at the prospect of such a ground-breaking development – to our knowledge, nobody had ever thought of doing anything like it at Le Mans and it was perfectly aligned with my thoughts about widening access to the team for the fans. There were thousands of people right around the world who would not be able to make the trip to France, but whom we knew would love to be a part of the action.

We soon ran into some problems. First, there was the very strict control of images from inside the circuit. The ACO, canny as ever in matters commercial, exercised a tight grip on this area. In a minor stroke of genius, we sailed straight over this fence – there was little or no restriction on the use of still pictures; how could anybody police 250,000 people with cameras? So we figured that a web cam, with a refresh rate of around twenty seconds, was effectively just a series of stills. We were in the clear.

More difficult to overcome was the simple matter of securing an ADSL line into the garage. This small but vital detail took many hours of time from myself, Natasha, Matthew's French-speaking assistant Samantha, Henri Sykowski, a French friend of Christopher's, and finally, the Paris-based French Morgan agents.

At last, we packed our bags and left for France, almost safe in the knowledge that the line would be installed and would be operational by the time we needed it.

Twenty-four hours is a long time to race a sports car. It's an act of supreme stamina from the team, the drivers and the support staff. Many of the fans who flock to the race don't stay up all through the race, preferring to crash out in varying stages of inebriation in their tents, the back of cars or anywhere else they can sleep it off for a few hours.

Many of the world's media can be found during the small hours with their heads down over their desks between the computer screens, relatively comfortable in the air conditioned, sound-proofed media centre.

For the team, the most they can hope for during the race is a few mini power naps between pit stops. Some have even perfected the art of sleeping standing up, their radio head sets on one ear so that they can instantly switch into action if a wake up call is sounded.

It's tough. What the outside world doesn't see are the endless days and nights of little or no sleep that batter and test the team even before the race starts. For the tiny Morgan Team, there were weeks of long days at the race shop, trying to prepare the car, the spares inventory and all the equipment that would have to travel first to Miramas and then up to Le Mans. An average day might involve up to 18 hours working, seven days a week.

Then, after a gruelling day of loading the truck, came the long journey down to Le Mans. Sleep came in small bites, grabbed in the truck or in an uncomfortable minibus seat. Arriving at the test site, there was just 4 hours sleep before getting set up. Time is money and therefore always in short supply.

Two long hard days of testing followed, with the huge luxury of one night in a hotel room in between.

Then came packing up and loading again and another long, slow drive back up through France to the Le Mans circuit. After squeezing the 30m truck into its allocated slot, two days of unpacking and set up followed. Race week was about to begin.

four

The long and winding road

In the role of PR manager for Morgan and, by proxy, also for the team at Le Mans, it was my job to brief everybody about what to expect at the big race and provide some guidance on how to handle it. From the media coverage and interest before the race, we already knew that interest would be feverish. Morgan's return to the famous circuit after an absence of forty years, along with all the other elements of the story that we had been working for several months to build, were certain to make the team the centre of a maelstrom. But nothing prepared any of us for the scenes that greeted us as the week unfolded and the crowds built up.

Inside the team, already pushed beyond any normal limits by the workload and lack of sleep, tensions were extreme. The clashes of ego and personality escalated as each hour passed and race day loomed large. Early in the week, the first big test came with scrutineering. This process involves a technical examination of the car to ensure that it meets the strict requirements of the rules. At most races, it involves maybe an hour of measuring and assessment, perhaps resulting in a few small discrepancies that the technical team is then required to fix and have signed off before the all-important race sticker is issued. Without this sticker, the car simply cannot race.

For Le Mans, like every other aspect of the event, scrutineering is raised to a state of high theatre. The car is transported from the circuit to the centre of the city, where a huge show is arranged in a garden. There are stages, jazz bands, bars, a market; a whole circus with thousands of people milling around.

The car, accompanied by a core team of technicians dressed up in the cleanest outfits they can muster, waits in line for its turn, surrounded by a throng of well-wishers and autograph hunters. When the time eventually comes, it goes into a roped-off area where the scrutineering proper begins.

I have a personal theory about the good people of Le Mans. Something in the air or the water, or maybe the genetic pool, gives them a burning desire to

The DeWalt/RSS Morgan Aero 8 is wheeled out for scrutineering. (Morgan Motor Company)

be policemen. And once a year they are given the chance to live out their dream very publicly. The officials, and there are many of them, seem actively to promote their own stereotype. Carefully groomed moustaches dominate, the size and flamboyancy of the hair arrangement maybe bearing some esoteric relationship to the relative importance of the individual. Naturally, there's a strict pecking order, from the lowly stewards who direct traffic and parking, to those that check passes, all the way up to the holy of holies – the race management itself.

Scrutineering is high theatre, or perhaps pantomime. Inside the cordoned area, a succession of these Very Important Individuals examines the car from every conceivable angle, using specially designed tools and equipment that add to the impression of some kind of weird Masonic ritual. They measure. They discuss, stroking moustaches meaningfully. They measure again. Heads shake. Heads nod. Hands gesticulate. The crowd looks on. The TV cameras try to catch every nuance.

For the team, it is an excruciating process. Any one of these officials has the power to end the dream of the entire team and all the fans – right there and then. And with little or no chance of appeal.

When one set of officials has finally finished, they add their notes to the documentation and the circus moves on a few metres to the next station, where the whole thing starts again, looking at a different area of the car's construction. For the DeWalt/Morgan Team, it was a very worrying 2 hours. Being so unusual and racing at Le Mans for the first time, the Morgan attracted microscopic attention from officials determined to demonstrate their virility.

We waited with bated breath at the end of the line, trying to glean some idea of how it was going from the expressions of the team and the officials. It was not going well. After an eternity, the Aero 8 was pushed out of the last of the scrutineering stations and into a large area in front of a grandstand packed with photographers. The team lined up behind the car and we pushed and shoved to get into position to get the shots we needed for our own purposes. Somehow I grabbed Steve Lawrence, who had been with the car throughout and asked him how it had gone.

'OK,' he said grudgingly. 'But we've got some work to do.' Just like his father, Steve was never a man for too many words.

There was just one day before the car would line up for the first qualifying session – but only if all the work demanded by the scrutineers was completed to their satisfaction.

Back at the circuit, the sound of power tools, hammers, grinders and cursing continued long into the night. The team finally threw in the towel around one o'clock. They were back at the circuit by 0630 in the morning. The sky was deep blue, not a cloud in sight. By nine in the morning, the temperature inside the metal box of the garage was over 35 degrees Celsius.

While the team worked flat out in the killing heat, they were required to do so in the full glare of attention from the crowd. Strict rules, enforced by big fines, demanded that the front door of the pit garage remained open at all times. The fans, often ten or more deep behind the rope barriers, craned for a view of the action, pushing and shoving for position. There were hundreds of Morgan fans, many of whom had made the trip especially to see the car. Natasha and I spent all day talking, re-assuring, building our story. The sun beat down relentlessly. By mid-afternoon, we were both hoarse.

Finally the scrutineers were happy. The all-important sticker was placed on the car. We were in the race – so long as we could make a qualifying time.

As dusk settled, the pit lane was cleared for action and soon the evening air was rent with the roar of thousands of horsepower as engines were warmed up. Activity in all the garages reached fever pitch. The elite pit crews, the ones who would work in the pit lane during the session, donned their compulsory safety gear – fireproof overalls, balaclavas, goggles and gloves. The ambient temperature hovered around the 35 mark.

Christopher Lawrence, a calm and studied presence among the controlled chaos, slowly made his way across his little perch on the pit wall, his clipboard and stopwatch striking a slightly incongruous note among all the high technology. The car was bristling with electronics, including an official timing system accurate to several fractions of a second. But Chris was well known for his cynical view of electronics. He was comfortable with his stopwatch.

Suddenly it was go. The pit exit lights went green and fifty of the world's best sports cars crackled and popped down the pit lane, their speed limiters holding them back until the final Marshall flagged them out onto the track and they roared and screamed off into the approaching night.

As soon as the car disappeared out of the pit lane, there was strangely little to see. The crew rushed back into the garage, eyes glued to the unreliable little TV screen high up on the wall. Now it was a numbers game.

The numbers were not good. After just a few laps, Richard Stanton was back in to the pits reporting vibration. The crew worked furiously under the rear of the car. Stanton went back out. The car was lapping at around 4 minutes 30 – not good enough. The other drivers, Steve Hyde and Richard Hay, both did a few laps to get their eye in. Neither could make much progress on the times. They were far from happy. The 2-hour session seemed to be over in a flash. There was a 1-hour break before the night session started. In the Morgan garage, nobody was resting as the crew worked to address initial feedback from the drivers.

2200 came round fast. The circuit was open, but the car was not ready. Valuable time was ebbing away. Finally, the Morgan roared off. For the first time, in the garage we heard a corresponding roar from the grandstands opposite the pit lane. We peered out, trying to see through the blinding lights. There were people over there. People cheering for Morgan.

The qualifying session ended at midnight. The team had not managed to make any significant progress and the Aero 8 was sitting firmly in last place in class. The mood was low. Groups of drivers and technicians huddled together. Blame and recrimination were thick in the air, like Gauloises smoke in a downtown bar. Work continued until around 0200. It was a quiet, subdued minibus that headed back to the chateau, where they could look forward to a full 4 hours of sleep.

Thursday dawned, another seering hot day in prospect. Today was crunch day and everyone knew it. The best lap time any one of the drivers had managed so far was 4 minutes 27 seconds. We needed to see at least 10 seconds off this to be sure of a qualified starting position in the race. It seemed a very tall order.

The team worked on the car all day again, the sun beating down mercilessly and the crowds even bigger than the previous day. Natasha and I had back-to-back interviews with media, some of them cynical, sensing a dramatic failure about to unfold in the Morgan camp. We kept positive. When you have told a positive story so many times, there's a real danger that you will begin to believe it yourself.

They were not all cynical, though, and as the afternoon heat peaked and began to slightly cool, well-wishers came by to lend moral support.

I grabbed the team moped and took off for a break from the madness. There's a real feeling of being in the epicentre of a storm in the pit garage. It becomes your whole, surreal world. Everything else in your 'normal' life – family, friends, business and all – fades into the background. You exist in a mad, frenetic bubble.

I drove around the public area outside the paddock. The world here had changed dramatically. Where there had been a few people milling about, now it was almost impossible to move through the crowds. The full impact of the public face of Le Mans hit me for the first time. Up on the hill, the funfair was in full swing. From this vantage point, camp sites and car parks stretched to the horizon. I sat at a bar and had a cold beer, trying to absorb it all. All for cars? It just didn't seem credible. Then, in a flash, I saw it all in a different light. I had seen this all before – of course I had. This was a pop festival. And just like at a pop festival, the centre stage bands were only a tiny fraction of the event. This was not really about cars at all. This was about people. People coming together, with some common references, but also to demonstrate and celebrate their differences. People were just as likely to remember what happened on the campsites as what happened on the track. This was a party. It was rock and roll. Now I felt a little more at home.

There was little time for more reflection. I finished the beer and fought my way back to the paddock. There were only minutes to go. The team worked frenetically to get the car out and this time it was ready on time. Green lights. Roar. TV screen.

Again all three drivers went out in rotation. And again the 4.27 time stuck stubbornly on the score board. It was looking bleak.

Richard Hay took the wheel just as it was getting dark. Backstage, out of sight of the crowd and the cameras, Richard Stanton, Dennis Leech and Christopher Lawrence were looking worried. For the first time, Natasha and I began to discuss how we would word a press release announcing a failure to qualify. Suddenly, there was a loud shout from inside the garage, followed quickly by a huge roar from the grandstands opposite. 4.16! Hay's done a 4.16! Incredulous, we all rushed in to fight for a view of the TV monitor. There it was, confirmed on the screen Morgan Aero 8, 4 minutes 16 seconds. The mood swing in the garage was amazing, all divisions forgotten for the moment as the reality sunk in.

I looked over at Christopher Lawrence. His face was as inscrutable as a Chinese sage. He carried on making notes on his clipboard.

Soon Richard Hay came in, to renewed cheering from the pit crew and the crowd. He had booked our place in the race. A crate of beer was produced and quickly dispensed. It was midnight. Richard Stanton gathered everybody around.

'Well done everyone,' he said quietly. 'Tomorrow will be the engine change.'

This may have been the moment when the full impact of endurance racing hit me. It is not the long races themselves – they are just the public tip of the iceberg. This team had averaged 4 hours sleep a day for almost a month. They had been at the circuit for six days already. A 24-hour race was due to start on Saturday. It was now midnight on Thursday. And tomorrow would be the engine change.

With the knowledge that qualification had been confirmed and that a good 10 hours of solid engineering slog lay in front of them in the morning, the team headed off to their favourite bar in Le Mans before hitting the sack around three o'clock.

Friday at Le Mans is a PR day. There is no track action and the cars should ideally be all polished up and on display to the public, while the technical team take an easy day before the race day and the drivers sign autographs and pose for photos before heading off into town for the big driver's parade in the evening.

In the Morgan garage, work started at 0800. The engine change on the Aero 8 is a long and complicated job that needs the whole front of the car to be stripped down.

Again the crowds were ten deep all day. And again, Natasha and I lost our voices talking to the enthusiasts in the hot sun. I had a quiet cup of coffee with Christopher Lawrence.

'Don't say a bloody word to anyone,' he murmured. 'But there's no way Hay did a 4.16.'

'What?'

'No way.' He repeated. He showed me his clipboard. It showed 4.27, 4.26, 4.27, 4.25....no 4.16. Nowhere. None.

'I never did trust those bloody electronic timers.' He growled.

My eyes may have nearly popped out of my head as I took on board the full implications of what he was telling me. Either the electronic timing was wrong, or Christopher's stopwatch was, or something or someone had intervened on Morgan's behalf to ensure a decent qualifying time. Christopher wandered off, muttering darkly to himself.

I quickly decided that this was one area where our open access policy would not apply.

David Morgan, the internet wizard from Morgan's web company Sure, had arrived late the night before to help get the web cam up and running. He turned out to have been the bearer of the crate of beer that refreshed us all after Hay's spectacular lap; further proof that David is one of the world's true gentlemen.

In all the excitement of qualifying, we had almost forgotten about our little internet surprise. It seemed that the France Telecom officials had forgotten about it completely: we still did not have a working ADSL line and without it, there would be no show. We deployed all our available resources to attack this problem. Anyone who could speak French was press-ganged and dispatched to the press room, the Organisers' office, the Telecom office, anywhere we could think of. We were promised that the line would be up and running by Friday evening.

David set up the web camera and the support systems – a small table tucked into a corner at the back of the garage would be our high-tech 'media centre' for the race. All that was left to do for him was to wait for France Telecom.

He waited. At 2130, we decided to give up. Tomorrow would be another day.

The engine change team was still working. I looked along the now empty pit lane. There were no lights on in any other garage. Morgan was the only team still working. The others, with their ample budgets for spare engines, had done their final polishing and were by now probably enjoying the party down town before getting a relatively early night.

Why do they do it, these race mechanics? Contrary to popular opinion, they do not earn vast fortunes – certainly not with the Morgan Team. Most are not paid by the hour. There are no unions here, no shop stewards, no paid holidays and no pension schemes. Working conditions are generally terrible. If the car does well, it's the drivers who get all the glory. If it runs badly, the mechanics take the rap. And yet there are always people queuing up for the jobs. Many volunteer, asking only for board and lodging. They just want to be part of it.

I can only comment on the Morgan Team and, specifically, the Morgan people. There was a deep passion here; a grim determination to prove their worth and that of *their* car. They were rightly proud. The more cynical the world was about their abilities, the more determined they were to prove their worth. And I think that is the key to understanding them. You could put aside legal niceties about who actually owned the nuts and bolts, the aluminium panels. There was no doubt in their minds – this was their car and no one was going to stop them. For their car, they would push themselves up to and beyond their limits of endurance. The Morgan badge was their rallying banner, but they did not salute it in the mindless way of a career soldier or a mercenary. Ultimately, they did it for themselves and that's why they could not be managed by any conventional method.

Watching them work so hard, so tirelessly and so determinedly was a humbling experience. Steve Lawrence, Dave Bradley, Mark Baldwin, John Burbidge: complex, gifted and flawed individualists, they somehow gelled with each other in their common mission. And they even managed an uneasy truce with the 'other' people; the ex-TVR technicians they were now working alongside. But when the chips were down and the new engine needed to go in and go in right, it was the Morgan men who took the vanguard.

There was nothing more David Morgan, Natasha and I could do that night and we left the circuit around 2200 for a quick meal and a few glasses of wine before hitting our beds, completely exhausted, around midnight.

God knows what time the mechanics finished. Later I heard that just before dawn, one of them was found collapsed in a corridor of the chateau. He was lying in a pool of vomit and his bowels and his bladder had spontaneously emptied. The others picked him up and cleaned him and the carpet. He was back in action at the circuit by 0700 the next day.

Race day. With up to a quarter of a million people converging on the circuit, the first problem was getting in. We set off early, but we were sat in a traffic jam by 0800. I had never seen a traffic jam quite like this one; with every other car a classic sports car or a charabanc full of partying people, it was more like a carnival.

Music blared from every vehicle and spirits were high. In the distance, coming down between the two lanes of stationary traffic, I saw a group of what looked like British policemen. As they got closer, I could see that while the top half of their bodies were indeed perfect London police uniforms, complete with 'tit top' hats, their bottom halves were pink ballet tutus – the whole outfit completed by pink tights and enormous police boots. They were swinging truncheons and handing out spoof traffic violation notices and enormous grins to the waiting cars as they proceeded down the line.

This surreal sight lifted my spirits and I eased unusually calmly into the waiting. It took around 90 minutes to cover three miles, but finally I was inside. For the first time, I fully realised that I was now in and there would be no going out again. It was 0930 on Saturday. If all went well, it would be well after 1600 the following day before I saw the outside world. Or saw a hot shower and a change of clothes.

At the pit garage, race preparations were in full swing. The logistics of keeping a 24-hour race team going are extraordinary. Food, clean clothes and above all, water are vital requirements and the team managers have to plan for the total impossibility of getting in and out of the circuit after around 1000 on race day.

It's a little known fact that a race team at Le Mans uses more water than it does fuel. With an ambient temperature reaching over 38C and some thirty people working for 36 hours, the water consumption is phenomenal. There is no drinking water on tap in the garage, so every drop has to be shipped in. At the back of the garage, a large dump of water bottles was stacked in every available corner. David Morgan and I fought our way through the piles and the unloading activity to locate our little IT corner. We found the ADSL junction box. It was still not working. We tried calling the mobile number we had been given for the engineer. There was no answer. We were stumped. We had run out of options.

Just as we were about to give up the idea of the first ever web cast from the Le Mans pits and start packing away the computer kit, the French engineer arrived. Cool and calm, he greeted us with a smile and a jolly 'Bonjour' and without apology or further conversation, he set to work with a small screwdriver on the junction box.

Five minutes later, he held out a form for us to sign, smiled again and said '*Il marche bien. Au revoir, messieurs!*'

With only hours to go, David Morgan set to work on the complex back-office set ups that would make the site and the web cam live.

Things were happening very quickly now. VIP guests arrived in streams – sponsors, Morgan shareholders, British TV and press people who had a special interest in the Morgan story. Natasha and I started ferrying press packs over to the press office. Two boxes at a time, about once every hour. We balanced them precariously on the back of the moped and then lugged up the two flights of stairs to the media centre. The centre was packed now, hundreds of journalists filing their early stories from their laptops. With its air conditioning, the centre was a welcome haven from the heat outside and after each delivery of press packs, we hung around for a while, seeking out the British media for a chat.

The ACO know better than anyone else in the game how to build an atmosphere. After almost a week of activity on and off track – the razzmatazz of scrutineering, the drama qualifying and the pomp of the drivers parade through the city – excitement builds to a fever pitch leading up to the start at 1600 on Saturday. The cars start assembling on the grid by 1330 for photocalls. The grandstands, sparsely populated during the previous week, are packed to capacity by 1500. The whole of the pit lane and the pit straight is jammed with cars, teams, media and team hangers-on; a seething mass of colour and movement. Somehow the area is cleared of all but the necessary crew members around ten minutes before the start. The stage is set. The French commentator reaches an orgasm of enthusiasm. We don't know what he's saying, but it's obviously exciting. Out of the clear blue sky, a fly past of French military jet aircraft swoops down low over the pit straight, painting red, blue and white stripes over the scene. The *Marsellaise* blares out of the Tannoy system. The crowd goes wild, blowing trumpets, whistles and klaxons, furiously waving flags and giant hands and letting off the occasional explosive flare.

Engines start. The cars roar off for the warm up lap in an incredible cacophony. A few minutes pass. The circuit is so long. Then the roar from the crowd builds again as the race leaders approach the pit straight. The lights go green. The engine noise raises up another pitch as full power is applied. The race is on!

An early unplanned pit stop. (DailySportsCar.com)

There's a little deflation after the start; the inevitable anti-climax. The crew retreated into the garage, eyes glued to the screen. I went up to the grandstand above the garage to watch the first few laps. The field was already strung out, with the front-running prototypes screaming ahead of the rest. But there were still 3 ½ minutes before any car came around – it was a long wait. The Morgan looked good and sounded wonderful. Something was wrong. There was no sign of the Aero 8 when I expected it. The car was in the pits. I rushed downstairs.

The vibration that Richard Stanton had complained about during qualifying was apparently back. The team couldn't find a problem. Stanton insisted that the rear axle needed changing. The team worked at a fantastic pace, replacing the whole rear end of the car in less than 30 minutes.

Suddenly there were media everywhere, thrusting microphones and clutching notebooks.

'There was some vibration from the back end,' Richard tells them. 'We took the decision to change it now, rather than risk a problem later on.'

Hyde and Hay put in their first sessions, with no reports of problems. Later, Stanton goes back out and pronounces the back end much better now.

Sometime after the race, Christopher Lawrence confided to me that the unit that replaced the one rejected by Stanton had been exactly the same as the one they took out. A complete breakdown of the suspect unit found no faults at all.

The race was well under way now and everyone began to settle in for the long night ahead.

Race day is what the teams live for. It is their day on stage; the glamour, the cameras and the crowd are their payback – for all the blood, sweat and tears. Spirits were high and the friendly banter showed that all barriers between the two camps were down; civil war hostilities suspended, for the moment, by the greater battle out on the circuit.

'The Le Mans 24 Hour race is a war of attrition,' Christopher had said to me in one of his rare moments of verbosity.

'Don't worry about how fast you're going. It's all about keeping going and about not spending time in the pits.'

As the first few hours came and went. I began to understand what he had been talking about. We watched the screen, at first constantly, then intermittently. The Aero 8 was circulating at or close to the planned race pace of 4 minutes 27. Conserving the mechanicals, minimising stress on the car and the drivers. We were far from being the fastest, even in our class. But before long, a couple of cars in front of us were no longer there – a split-second driver error here, a broken drive shaft there. Hit the wall, or break down on the track and you're out of the race, unless you can limp back unaided to the pits.

In the early hours of the race, heat was the number one enemy. The ambient temperature on the track rose to 39C around 1800, 2 hours into the race. Tyres began to melt. So did drivers. As Steve Hyde came in after one session, he almost

The Morgan's strange looks and the spirit of the team stole the hearts of the 2002 crowd. (Morgan Motor Company)

collapsed from heat exhaustion. I was quite worried about him, but he gradually recovered, sitting quietly at the back of the pit garage sipping water.

The data downloads showed heat too. Heat in the engine, the gearbox, the transmission tunnel and the differential. Too much heat. Heat increases the stress on all metal parts, rapidly hastening their eventual failure. There was nothing that could be done except keep the pace down and pray for nightfall and cooler air.

Night came. Nothing compares with the first sight of a Le Mans race at night time. Out of the darkness, the cars scream into view for a split second, flames belching from exhausts and brake discs glowing bright red as the drivers change down and brake for the bend at the end of the pit straight. I watched for some time from the grandstand, picking out the Morgan long before it came into sight from its deep, distinctive exhaust roar.

Round and round. After 6 hours or so, the whole thing takes on a surreal aspect. Everyone is praying for nothing to happen, nothing untoward. There's the occasional moment of excitement as one of the cars in front of us breaks down and then gets going again. Meals and endless cups of coffee come and go. Every 90 minutes, the car is in the pits for fuel, tyre change and sometimes a driver change. Then there's frantic activity for 3 or 4 minutes. The car roars off and everybody settles down again. The wiser, more experienced campaigners in the team rest their tired feet and legs at every opportunity. The younger ones, fuelled by excitement and the presence of the live web cam, are frisky, putting on impromptu entertainments for the cameras.

Midnight approached. We wrote an 8 hours press release and took it over to the media centre. One wall there was taken up with a large chart detailing all the cars. We browsed over it, noting the growing number of retirements. Engine failures, crashes, electrics… each told a story of its own and I pondered on the human stories, the effort, the money and the nail biting that had sadly ended already for many.

But the important thing was that the Morgan was still running. This became a mantra as we bumped into many people we knew; journalists, other teams, other PRs.

'You still running?'

'So far, so good. Long way to go.' This was the only acceptable reply.

Back at the camp, Matthew and David were doing a fantastic job with the web cam and race reports. Matthew was posting brief updates on the web bulletin board every few minutes and incoming emails and messages of support showed that we had a truly global audience. People were with us at home in the UK, right across Europe, in the USA and even further flung countries; we saw Malaysia, Australia, New Zealand and even Russia represented. It was a fantastic feeling to know that so many people were right there with us.

Buoyed by passing the 8 hours stage, the pit crew were ever more frisky. Somebody set up an impromptu Twister board on the floor of the garage and the crew entertained the web audience and the circuit TV with hilarious live action. It was a small demonstration of the unique spirit and humour that stood the Morgan Team apart from the rest. The host of Porsche teams, most of them still running like clockwork, seemed sad and soulless in comparison – an extension of the difference in engineering style between the cold and clinical 911s and the organic, impossible Aero 8.

Out on the pit wall, Christopher Lawrence was implacable. He chewed a sandwich, sipped a coffee and religiously noted down every single lap time as the Morgan roared past. The grandstands had thinned out, but directly opposite the garage, a small but very vocal group of Morgan fans cheered and honked and waved every time the car came in for a pit stop. As the car went back out yet again, the crew lined up across the garage entrance and took a pantomime bow before waving to the fans and giving them a very British thumbs-up.

Sometime around 0200, Stanton reported bad vibration again. The car was brought into the garage and once again the team worked furiously fast to change the whole back end. They completed the work in a stunning record time of just 14 minutes. The car was back on track. The crowd opposite went berserk. The team took another bow.

The hours till dawn seemed to go by very quickly. As the eastern sky showed its first glint of light, I took the moped and rode out to the Porsche curves to watch for a while. I had been on the circuit for more than a week and this was the first time I had the opportunity to see anything but the pit straight and the media centre. It was an awesome sight. In the growing, clear light of the dawn of another cloudless day, the cars seemed glued to the racing line. Brakes glowed red and orange. The Morgan looked beautiful.

Around me were groups of die-hard fans, some who had just woken up after a few hours in their tents, others who seemed to have stayed up all night, wrapped in blankets against the cold of the night. Many raised a wave and a cheer every time the Morgan went past. The drivers told me later that this had gone on all night, all around the long circuit.

Suddenly it was morning. Fresh coffee and croissants refreshed the team. Those who had had the forethought to come prepared found time for a quick shower and brush up.

'Still running?' People kept coming by, their questions increasingly tinted with amazement.

'So far so good. Long way to go.' Like a mantra.

Fourteen hours were behind us. There were still another 10 hours of racing to go, but surely we were over the hill? Some of us began to think the impossible. Hundreds of messages of support were coming in by email and on the web site message boards. The web statistics showed that some 6,000 people had visited us during the night. Many were still there. People in the USA were watching the race on satellite TV and via our web site at the same time. They loved it. Some friends from the MG PR team came over for a coffee. We showed them what we were doing and they couldn't believe that neither they or any of the other teams, for all their enormous resources, had thought of doing something similar. Matthew Parkin positively glowed at the huge success that had grown out of his original, inspired idea. We offered to relieve him for a while, but he was glued to the little notebook PC, huddled in an impossibly small corner and would not leave his post. He was having a real ball.

As the sun rapidly warmed up, David Morgan and I walked a short distance to a bar to get coffee and pastries. We sat chatting in the sunshine, daring to envisage finishing the race. Surely we were over the hill? It was approaching 0900.

I can't remember what alerted us to a problem. Suddenly we were back at the garage and in an instant we knew something was badly wrong. The team, which seconds before had been smiling and drinking hot coffee in the sun, were highly animated now, listening intently to their headsets. I tried to find out what was up. The screen told the tale: 'Car No.73 slow on circuit.' Whatever it was, it was serious. If Richard could not make it back to the pits, we were finished. Information flew around the garage. Engine failure. The worst possible news. But he was limping along. Could he make it?

He was coming in. Frantic preparations were made in the garage. Instructions were screamed out. Mechanics, who had been up all night and had little sleep for weeks, sprinted in and out of the race truck, grabbing tools and spares. There was a huge crowd of people at the back of the garage. They were brusquely shoved out of the way in the rush. We cleared a path and tried to rope it off.

Richard made it. The car came into the garage front in – the first time I had seen it do so. In seconds it was raised up on its jacks, the bonnet and front body panels were off and the senior mechanics were huddled around the engine. The support crew stood back, passing in tools as they were called for, looking for all the world like a surgical team.

The patient was dying. The engine specialist from Mader arrived, their detached calmness a harsh contrast to the Morgan Team's desperate anguish. They looked into the engine compartment, shining torches into the smoking innards. They called for more components to be stripped out. Again the mechanics worked frantically.

I caught sight of Christopher Lawrence. He had come in from the pit wall and was watching calmly from a short distance. His face was grim. He constantly looked at his watch. The top of the engine was now laid bare. The Mader men looked again. I saw one shake his head. One of the Morgan mechanics hit the car hard as if to say, 'You can't die, don't you die on me, you bastard.'

The surgeons straightened up, their faces drained of blood. It was over.

The people who do this stuff are hard, tough, mean individuals; they are testosterone personified. But in the minutes that followed, all the weeks and months of effort, of fighting the impossible fight, of getting so close to achieving their dream, shattered them completely. They cried. Like babies. Some wept openly, tears making tracks down their grimy faces. Others disappeared to grieve in private. Tears welled in my own eyes. People were hugging each other.

I sat down at the computer to write the press release I had never wanted to write. People were crowding around me, looking over my shoulders at the words that I was typing.

'After 17 hours of glorious running and a superhuman effort from the Morgan Team….'

The emotion overwhelmed me. I broke down, shouting at the crowding people indiscriminately.

'Just give me space, please!'

Two days and almost a thousand miles of driving later, I arrived at my family's holiday home in Cornwall. My wife George greeted me with a hug.

'How was it?' she asked

'Well, it was life changing, actually,' I replied, trying not to be over-dramatic.

'Don't be silly,' she said. 'It's only a motor race.'

PART TWO

On a Mission

five

'We're going to need some sponsorship'

I spent the short holiday recovering physically and mentally from the emotional rollercoaster of Le Mans. After a few days, the noise of race cars, which had invaded even my sleep, faded from my head, replaced by the more beneficial gentle rhythm of the sea crashing on the shore. I built sandcastles with my two-year-old son and flew a kite on the beach. But mostly I looked quietly at the sea. Eventually, a form of normality returned.

Back at the office all too soon, we picked up the aftermath. The post race publicity had been very positive, despite the team's ultimate failure to finish. For once, we had persuaded at least some people that it really was the taking part that counted. The Morgan name had not been so visible for many years.

The constant round of press releases, photography session and TV crew visits to the Malvern factory recommenced. Life was getting back to normal.

Among those at the factory who had been involved – either as members of the team or as spectators – there was already talk of 'Next year'. 'Unfinished business', somebody said.

Christopher Lawrence had produced several pages of hand-written notes about what went wrong and what was needed to do better. He identified ways to shave several seconds off the car's lap times and outlined the technical programme required to achieve it. The document was circulated to Morgan's senior management. There was little or no reaction. Irrepressible as ever, Christopher threw himself into a new project. He had produced a specification for a 'Cup' class racing version of the Aero 8 – a development of the road car designed to compete in national racing. Soon, he had an order for two of these cars from a customer in the USA and they quickly started to take shape in the race shop.

I discussed the whole racing project with Charles. I believed that Le Mans and the potential of the new Cup cars could help to demonstrate the technical credibility of the Aero 8 to a young, international audience. This was directly in line with my original brief and we believed it to be important because there was still such a strong background of cynicism. Morgans were stuck with an image of being quaint, old-fashioned cars for eccentric people. It had taken over ninety years to establish this reputation; it was not going to be easy to change it.

Exposure of the Morgan brand on a corporate level was also a very valid objective and as we reviewed the huge TV, radio and printed media coverage that Le Mans had generated, it was obvious that a lot had been achieved. The worldwide Morgan community had also been invigorated by the team's escapades, but this was perhaps even more difficult to quantify and evaluate as a benefit to the company.

There was strong resistance within the Morgan family shareholders to the whole idea of racing. They had good cause to be cautious. Back in the 1960s, when Christopher Lawrence was winning races in a Morgan, there was a lot of truth in the old adage 'win the race on Sunday, sell more cars on Monday'. Times had changed. Now, unless you could measure it, it probably wasn't so. With his huge experience, the venerable chairman, Peter Morgan, knew better than most how expensive motor sport could be. Notwithstanding the publicity that had been generated simply by taking part, the point of racing must primarily be to win. And we were a million miles and potentially several million pounds away from winning.

There was a lot of discussion about what Richard Stanton would do next. The financial situation had become murky as the full costs of the party in France unfolded and arguments developed about who should pay what for which elements. The simple fact was that neither Morgan nor Stanton's DeWalt-sponsored team would have made it to the race without each other. This made it a partnership, but without a formal agreement there were simply too many grey areas. Who had gained what and how much had each party contributed? No contracts. No resolutions.

Like everything else I had so far encountered in my brief sojourn with motorsport, nothing was clear-cut. Certainly Richard Stanton was a complex character. .

He had received an undisclosed sum from DeWalt to sponsor the Le Mans project. Despite the *de facto* partnership with Morgan that had made the event happen, there was no transparency; we were never party to any budget figures.

The rows about payment rumbled on, becoming increasingly sour. Nonetheless Richard dangled a juicy new carrot; maybe DeWalt would sponsor a 2003 campaign. He asked Christopher to start thinking about a specification for a new car.

I spoke to both Charles and Christopher and gave them my view, based on everything I had observed. In essence, Richard Stanton had always been a TVR man. He had come to Morgan for one reason only: TVR did not have a car at that time that would gain an entry at Le Mans. TVR were known to be working on a possible entry for 2003. The DeWalt money would follow Stanton where-ever he went and my guess was that he would announce a 2003 campaign with TVR before very long. If there was to be a Morgan entry in 2003, it would have to be on a different footing.

Christopher's new Cup cars were looking good and, on paper at least, very competitive. Charles was excited about them and came up with an inspired idea. Each race car would be produced in the same livery – a dark blue and silver two-tone. This would have the effect of making racing Aero 8's stand out wherever they appeared and in time they would seem to be everywhere.

It was around this time that Christopher first became ill. It began with what appeared to be a persistent cold and swollen glands, but before long it was diagnosed as a form of cancer of the lymphatic system. He started a long programme of chemotherapy, which he said was much worse than the illness itself. He soon lost his hair and was thereafter always seen with a flat cap. He refused to stop working.

I wrote to Charles, outlining my view that a 2003 entry for Morgan should be sought as a fully-fledged 'Works' team. I believed that after the huge impact in June, we should be able to generate substantial sponsorship to help with the costs. In a sentence that truly did change my life, I also suggested that I could take on the job of team manager if such a project went ahead.

Charles did not reply formally. When I next bumped into him at the factory, he simply acted as if it was a done deal. 'We are going to need some sponsorship,' was his only comment on the matter or my letter. It seemed that I had talked myself into a job.

As a PR exercise, we took the DeWalt Le Mans car to the Goodwood Festival of Speed. In the elite surroundings of the Driver's club, I arranged a radio interview for Charles. While he was in the tiny studio, I waited outside, looking with interest at some stunning black and white graphics that decorated the Dunhill-sponsored marquee. When Charles emerged, I pointed out the graphics.

'Don't you think Dunhill would make a perfect sponsor for the Morgan Le Mans Team?'

'Do you know, I think they would! And what's more, I'm having a coffee with just the man.'

Charles led me to one of the large round tables, where I was introduced to the wonderfully named Yann De Belle De Montby, Head of Corporate Communications for Dunhill.

After a few mild pleasantries, Charles turned to Yann.

'I don't suppose you want to sponsor our race team, do you?'

I was bowled over. But Yann, a perfectly studied and immaculately dressed gentleman, simply smiled warmly.

'You know, we just might.' He said, in a seductive French accent. 'Why don't you come and see us in London?'

Over the next few weeks, I worked fast to collate the materials we would need to support sponsorship presentations. You can't turn up to the headquarters of a company like Dunhill, show them a few dog-eared photographs and ask for a couple of million pounds. We commissioned Richard Hay, who as well as being one of the star drivers from the DeWalt team, was the owner of a well-known video business, to produce a video short. He did a fantastic job, cutting together footage of the car on track everywhere except the Le Mans race – and so avoiding prohibitive charges – with archive footage and crowd shots. It captured a lot of the atmosphere and provided us with a great starting point.

There are as many reasons why people sponsor racing cars as there are cars going around race circuits all over the world. At every level, from the top international events to the lowliest club meeting, people are sponsoring. Their reasons range from the purely scientific, well-resourced, professionally planned and executed marketing based on demographics and audience reach equations, through the blatantly emotional to the frankly ludicrous, with every degree in between.

Some sponsors in the emotional and ludicrous categories may go to great lengths to disguise their activities as scientific and there is often a great deal of bluster and bullshit to accompany what is effectively a decision based on pure sentiment.

When I was a young, green and very enthusiastic PR executive back in the late 1980s, I remember working on a campaign for one of the early mobile phone companies. This was at a time when mobile phones were the size of a shoe box and weighted several kilos. It seems unbelievable now, but a large part of my brief then was to generate application stories – trying to persuade an unsuspecting public that they needed a mobile telephone. Even in those early days, the company was awash with cash and when I joined the team they were already sponsoring a team in the British F3 Championship.

After a few months of PR duty at the circuits, a review meeting was called and I duly turned up with my report and recommendations. I listened to others giving glowing reports about how well it was all going. Then it was my turn. I so wanted to make an impression.

I passed around copies of the report and then summarised it for the meeting. The gist of the presentation was that the company was wasting its time spending money on F3. The demographics were all wrong, the tone of voice and the media routes inappropriate... in short, I was sure that if they switched the considerable funding they were 'wasting' on F3 to more creative PR under our remit, I was certain that we could deliver better and more cost-effective results.

The senior client managers listened politely to my speech. Then the marketing director said calmly and with some amusement, 'Thank you, David, that's all very interesting. But the chairman's wife loves F3, OK? Now, shall we move on to next season's plans?'

Of course, it's not always like that. When big, professional campaigns are executed – examples might be John Player before the tobacco ban and Red Bull more recently – they spend money precisely where it is going to have the maximum impact. Closer to home, I had been very impressed with the way in which DeWalt had made the 2002 Le Mans project work so well for them.

Firstly, they had a clear objective – to raise their brand profile across a pan-European audience of males aged 24-40. The demographics and audience reach of Le Mans were perfect for them and because they were after a pan-European profile, the relatively low attention given to the event by the UK media did not matter a great deal to DeWalt.

Second, with extensive experience of motorsport in the USA, they knew that if the project was going to work for them they would need a sustained effort. The Morgan DeWalt team was only a part of a three- or four-year programme of increasingly high profile European motorsport. Next, they allocated enough resource to make it work. With what was effectively a title sponsorship agreement for the Le Mans team, their powerful branding was everywhere – the car, the truck and the team. They went further still and supported the race team itself with a major promotional campaign before and during the race itself.

At the other end of the spectrum, there are any number of small, local companies and individuals who will hand over a few hundred pounds for the sake of an invitation to the paddock. They are the foot soldiers who keep motor sport running from the grass roots up.

With this insight, knowledge and experience on board, I was in no doubt that we could persuade someone to work with us for mutual benefit.

Hindsight is such a painful luxury. As we worked to build the proposals to sponsors, it seemed that it could only be a matter of time before somebody saw what a truly fantastic opportunity was on offer. Association with the powerful – and quintessentially British – Morgan brand with all its wonderful heritage and mythology, a well-defined international audience of wealthy owners and fans, high-profile media attention that could, uniquely for a motorsport team, break into mainstream national and international media, a really hot PR team driving it through... it was all there for the taking. There were no takers.

Whether the lack of big sponsors coming forward was a comment on my presentational skills, the strength of the arguments I deployed, the weakness of the resources we had available, a general malaise in sports sponsorship or perhaps the inability of most of British industry to see beyond the next set of accounts is a matter for conjecture. Not for the first or the last time, it was sheer self belief – and not much else – that carried us forward. I set out to enlist the help of specialist agencies who made a living out of finding sponsorship. Those that knew at least something about Morgan were receptive and we were encouraged by their positive response.

Of course it was the soft targets that everyone went for. There were any number of companies who wished to access the production operations at the Morgan factory to sell in their own products. More often than not, these deals were tied into future production volumes and so were very difficult to achieve given the very low output of hand-built cars from Malvern. Some money was found this way, though, and it was just enough to keep the build of the 2003 race car on track.

I was a little more successful with the driver line-up. Between Christopher and myself, we managed to persuade Charles Morgan that he should drive for the team. What a fantastic story it would make! It had been a very long time indeed since anyone had driven any car at Le Mans that carried his own family's name on the badge. Joining him would be Matt Griffin, a young and fast rising star from the British GT Championship, and Martin Short, one of the best known and best liked drivers on the British motorsport scene. It was a great result which brought in some much needed funds and a lot of good PR.

The best Morgan driver line that never was: Martin Short (left) and Matt Griffin, with Charles Morgan at the rear. (Morgan Motor Company)

six

'Sorry about the roof, mate!'

By now I had moved into a small office on site at the factory in order to be close to the day-to-day operations. I was still trying to run my PR business as well, so the plan was that I would spend two days a week at Malvern. It soon became clear that seven days a week was more realistic. As I learned more about what had transpired already and what was needed for the future, I was blown away by the incredible costs of the project. Hard-won funding from various small sponsors was invariably already spent even before the cheque arrived. The car was being built by hand from the ground up and every component cost a small fortune. Long hours were being worked by Steve Lawrence and his small team – and the inevitable big wages bills followed.

A meeting was arranged with senior management at Morgan to discuss progress and future planning. Charles re-iterated that the Board would not sanction any direct funding for the project. I should emphasise that Charles was personally as enthusiastic and excited as anyone about the Le Mans campaign. But Morgan is essentially a very small company with a very big brand. Every spare resource was already committed to the development of the Aero 8 road car. American federal approval, a vital step for the long-term success of the new car, was sucking up well over £1 million of hard-earned cash. This followed an estimated £2 million that had already been spent on developing the new car and there was simply nothing left to support a race team, no matter how well the case for it was made.

It was agreed that we would renew efforts to persuade more sponsors on board and the Board sanctioned the sale of some bits and pieces of old racing kit, which would also help. By the skin of our teeth, we were still in business.

I called all the sponsorship people again. They had no news. There were various explanations; we were asking way too late in the year, Le Mans had no profile in the UK (could no one think internationally in British marketing departments?), people don't like motorsport unless it's F1, etc. It was all very frustrating.

I decided that one of my first moves as 'team manager' would be to have some sort of team-building exercise. All concerned were invited to a curry and some beers. I laid on a minibus and a driver – my brother-in-law Tim FitzGerald – to ensure no one was tempted to drink and drive. The early part of the evening went well. I explained what I had in mind for the project and assured them all that things would be run differently than they had been in 2002. Firstly, it would be our own show and secondly, I promised that I would be a listening leader. This was well received, by all expect one individual. John Burbidge, a talented but rather volatile mechanic, was well the worse for wear half way through the evening and became more aggressive as time went on.

It was not easy to see the root of his problems, but it seemed related somehow to an inability to accept any authority from anyone. Trying to calm things, I had to explain that being listened to would not necessarily lead to his views always prevailing. The atmosphere was deteriorating quickly and I called a halt early, despite the fact that several of the team were keen to continue the party.

The minibus duly turned up to take people home, most of them to the Malvern area. I was staying at a friend's flat in town, so I walked there, pondering what I had just witnessed and what I was going to do about it. An hour or so later, Tim called me. He sounded shocked and subdued. There had been a fight in the minibus, he explained calmly. John had apparently lost the plot and lashed out at Mark Baldwin, who had been a close friend of John prior to this incident. There had been blood.

I was so sorry for Tim – dealing with this was in no way part of his job. I was also shocked and horrified that we were beginning a long hard road on such a disharmonious note. A great team-building result.

Later I saw some positive aspects. Clearly there had been poison in the group and at least we had drawn it into the open. There was to be formal disciplinary action at the factory, which involved the union and the factory management. John was suspended pending enquiries. It was absolutely clear that, whatever happened to him regarding his employment with Morgan, there could be no place for him with the Works race team. It was such a shame to lose a character and an excellent mechanic, but we could not risk such volatility in the cauldron of endurance races.

Our application for a 2003 entry at Le Mans was sent in, along with the considerable fee that must be lodged with it. With no funds and no car ready, we were forced to watch from a distance as the Sebring 12 Hour race in Florida went ahead without the Morgan Works Team. We knew that not being there could harm the case for our entry, but Christopher Lawrence was confident that the fantastic reception at Le Mans for the Morgan in 2002 and his personal relationships with the senior officials were certain to secure an invitation. While all this activity and effort was going on to try to get a Le Mans campaign off the ground, there was a development in the British GT which was to produce a very significant liaison.

One of Christopher's Cup Class Aero 8s had already been ordered by Keith Ahlers, a well-known Morgan aficionado and customer who planned to run it as a privateer entry in the British GT Championship. With the first race of the season at Donington Park just weeks away, Christopher was approached by Richard Thorne, one of Morgan's more successful British dealers, who wanted to enter a second car. This was very good news. Morgan had never had even one car entered in the national championship – the idea of two Aero 8s racing each other was a highly attractive one.

There were a few problems. Firstly, while a second Cup Class chassis was sitting in the race workshop on trestles, it had yet to feel a spanner. Second, there were only a few weeks to go before the first race. And third, Richard could not raise the full commercial asking price for the car.

Once again, emotion and sheer will took over where reason left off. We should have written it off as a nice idea, but not feasible. Maybe try again next season. But Christopher badly wanted a second car out there. So did Charles, who could see the potential benefits of two Aeros racing together. So did I – I thought the PR opportunities were significant and I could see potential knock-on benefits for our Le Mans programme too. The more visible we were, the better.

Somehow, a deal was done. Somehow, it was built in time, by a small dedicated team working on the new Cup car alongside to its slowly evolving Le Mans big sister.

The last bolt was secured at about ten thirty on the night before the first qualifying session was due at Donington. It was pushed out of the workshop and into the ubiquitous Morgan race box and delivered direct to the circuit early the following morning.

I went along to keep an eye on things. In Richard Thorne's pit garage, I was introduced to a cheeky-faced New Zealander, Neil Cunningham, who was to be one of Richard's drivers for the weekend. Neil had never seen an Aero 8, let alone driven one. He was champing at the bit to get on the track in it.

The free practice session started. The Cup car was fired up. Neil jumped in, adjusted the mirrors and shot off from the pit lane, quickly disappearing around the first turn.

Very shortly afterwards, he reappeared, storming down the pit straight. We all looked out as the car burned past… without a roof. Somewhere on the car's inaugural lap it had parted company with the car. Neil hadn't even slowed down.

He came in after a few laps, grinning from ear to ear, like a kid a Christmas. 'Sorry about the roof, mate!' He said, as if it was his fault that it had not been bolted down properly in the rush.

The roof was retrieved but was too badly damaged to be refitted. There was no spare. Special dispensation was sought and gained to allow the car to race without a roof. 'Now it's a proper bloody Morgan,' grunted Christopher.

The race was a real blinder. Neil and his co-driver Keith Robinson blasted the open-top car into second in class and seventh in the race overall. Keith Ahlers

Pit stop action at Donington Park. (Morgan Motor Company)

and his team mate Rob Wells were right with them, finishing third in class. It was a very exciting turning point. For the first time ever, two Morgan Aero 8's had competed in a British national event and both had won podium honours.

It was also the first time I ever saw Christopher Lawrence really happy. In the paddock after the race, his old adversary Dennis Leech came over to say hello. 'What have you done to make that old heap of shit go faster then, Chris?' He grunted. 'I kept your bloody hands off it, Dennis!' Christopher fired back, not losing a second. Two men in their late sixties, sparring like boys in the playground.

For the first time for decades, a Morgan had been right on the heels of the class-winning Porsche GT3. Not only that, but Richard Thorne's new car had quite literally come 'Out of the box and on to the podium,' as the press release was headlined. And not only that. Though I had no idea at the time, I had just met the racing driver who was to inspire, entertain and excite me all the way to the finishing line at Le Mans.

I was now sucked into the British GT Championship as well as the Le Mans campaign. With races every two weeks through the spring, summer and autumn all over the UK, it added a substantial additional strain on my family life. Added to testing and other commitments with the Works team, for the next several months there were to be very few weekends when I was not working at least some of the time.

Charles Morgan sheepishly announced one morning that he could not take on the Le Mans drive after all; things were just too busy at the factory, and he simply wasn't going to have time to bring his international licence up to date. I began looking for another driver in earnest.

Throughout the increasingly violent storm that was developing around us, my trusted assistant and protégé Natasha had been a vital support in keeping the day-to-day PR operations for Morgan and our other clients going smoothly. But she had been growing up even faster than I had realised. I always knew it could only be a matter of time before somebody snapped her up for a top job, but I had hoped it would be a little while yet. When she called she sounded full of excitement and sadness in equal measure; she had been offered a really good international PR job for a major manufacturer. I was genuinely delighted for her. But quite sad for myself – I was going to miss her. Luckily, another colleague, who had been with us for some time, was quickly able to fill Natasha's shoes. Maddy Phelps knew her way around motorsport and was a great help to me when the chips were down – as they all too often were.

When the full entry list for Sebring was published, we were a little surprised to see the DeWalt Morgan included. Richard Stanton was also listed, back to driving his beloved TVR. No drivers were listed for the Morgan. It seemed that Richard was taking something of a flier. As race weekend approached, it became clear that nobody had come forward with the required cash to drive the Morgan and the rather sad news reached us that the DeWalt Morgan was very publicly parked up in the paddock with a 'for sale' sign on its windscreen. This was not going to help our case with the ACO at all.

We were far too busy to dwell. Work on the car was behind schedule. Every pound we brought in was being spent three times over and there was still an enormous hole in our plans. Even if we completed the car, we needed somehow to fund some testing and then the Le Mans test weekend and the race itself. I was now spending every waking hour talking to potential sponsors.

seven

The Morgan Way

Early one afternoon in March, I left the little office and walked over to the race shop to discuss something with Steve Lawrence. As we were talking, I noticed a single page fax had arrived. I picked it up, glanced at it and quickly brought the conversation to a close. The contents of the fax had hit me hard in the guts and I surely must have turned white as I read it. I went back to the office, closed the door and read the single page note again and again.

The letter was from the ACO. It read as follows:

'Dear Mr Lawrence,

The Sporting Committee recently met to consider applications for an entry in 2003. I regret to tell you that on this occasion Morgan has not been selected for an entry.

Yours sincerely
Michael Cosson, President'

My heart froze. I simply could not believe what my eyes were telling me.

I called Christopher Lawrence. 'You'd better come in to the factory, Chris.'

He read the fax quietly. 'What the hell has gone wrong, Chris?' I asked.

'I really don't know,' he replied. For the first time, he seemed a totally beaten man. He looked very ill, pale, wan and fragile. He didn't even have an opinion. For the first time, it entered my mind that Christopher might die before too long. At the same instant, I became even more determined that we should take his car back to Le Mans before his time came.

Christopher immediately tried to reach someone at the ACO office, but no one was available. There was nothing we could do. But we simply had to know the reasons behind this bombshell. We were full of fight, but in our hearts I think we already knew it was final. The ACO is not required to explain. Their word is final. There is no appeal mechanism. The successful teams would have been informed by now and the fifty places were gone. That was it.

We gathered the team together in the race shop and told them the news, Christopher and I sharing the extremely difficult task. I searched desperately for suitable words. 'Look, we will do everything possible to find out why, but the main thing now is that we just can't give up. We have a race car. It's got to go racing. And we just have to make sure we get in next year. What we're going to do is to tick every fucking box the ACO gives us.'

Even as I spoke, I had no idea how, where or when this was going to come to pass. But I knew that if I left any doubt in their minds, the team would quickly dissipate. Steve Lawrence would go back to America, Rogier Vancamelbecke back to Belgium and Ben Coles back to Mars. They were like motorsport mercenaries. Passionate about what they did and consummately skilled, they would go to wherever the next action was. Not for the first time, nor the last, Morgan's Le Mans dream hung by a thread. No one could carry on working that day; it was time we all went to a local pub to drown our sorrows.

At home later that evening, my mind was racing faster than Neil Cunningham at Donington. There was so much to think about. Sponsorship deals would unravel. Refunds of money would be demanded. Oh God!... a potential major new sponsor was due to visit the next morning. It was far too late to cancel. How would we handle the announcement? What about the Exclusive Partners? There was something else... and it was very urgent.

I had been negotiating with a number of potential paying drivers as a replacement for Charles. The financial contribution would be vital and these negotiations were always very tricky. Steve Hyde, who had done such a sterling job for the DeWalt Morgan Team in 2002, was one of the leading contenders. I knew he was on the verge of signing a complicated deal that possibly involved driving in the British GT Championship with a private Morgan Team. The Le Mans drive was a critical element in his plans. I could not let another minute go by.

I called Steve immediately and broke the news, asking for complete confidence and knowing that I could totally rely on him for it.

The following days and weeks were among the worst of my working life. There was so much to do. We tried to prioritise. The new sponsors duly arrived the next day and we had a very different meeting than the one that had been planned. They took it very well, leaving hopeful doors open for the future.

The paying drivers were a different matter; they would have to take their resources elsewhere and try to find a drive. They needed their money back, and quickly. Most of it was already spent. It was all a terrible nightmare that didn't stop when I woke up each morning.

We met with Charles and the other Morgan directors immediately afterwards. After agreeing that we should do everything possible to find out what lay behind the shock news and whether there was the slightest hope of reversing the decision, we then considered what to do next. We'd come this far running largely on pure determination. I made an impassioned plea that we should fight on.

The choice was really quite simple. Close the project down, or find another suitable race. A great deal of money had already been spent. The car was virtually ready. Stopping now would simply write it off and we would surely never get another campaign off the ground. If we could only continue somehow, surely we would get the sponsors we needed. And in any case, giving up was not the Morgan way.

The FIA's Spa 24 Hour race, held in Belgium in August, was clearly the next available event. It would be second best, but a pretty good one. And before that, the FIA calendar included a 1,000 km race at Donington Park – home territory and virtually on our doorstep. The die was cast.

eight

Paperwork

Nothing is ever simple in this game. We had effectively died twice already – once on the track at Le Mans after 17 hours and again when the fax arrived from France. Now, clinging on to new life by our fingernails, we faced a torturous ordeal by regulations.

The car had been built for one purpose; to satisfy the ACO scrutineers and race at Le Mans. But the two races we had now signed up for were run under a completely different set of technical rules. It quickly became clear that we had a lot of work to do and not much time. In the race shop, the lights burned long into the night and weekends ceased to exist as Steve Lawrence and his team struggled to come to terms with a work list that covered several pages.

Meanwhile, the shock waves from that dreadful fax continued to reverberate. I issued a press release the day after we received the news. As expected, within an hour or so the phone lines were hot and emails were arriving in hundreds. People were genuinely incensed and it went deep. Among the British fans, the centuries-old rivalry between England and France was re-awoken. Across the Atlantic, where anti-French sentiment was rooted in recent and far more serious events, the many American Morgan supporters were even more vociferous.

Everyone wanted to know why. Everyone demanded an immediate reversal of the decision. But most of all, they wanted to vent their feelings. Emotions were running so high that I began to worry about the outcome. We were still determined that the only race we really wanted to run was Le Mans and it would not help our case in the long term if the ACO was bombarded with rude and offensive missives from angry Morgan fans. But we were not going to go completely quietly.

I suggested to anyone who was interested that they might like to write to the ACO and politely express their disappointment that Morgan had not been invited. To their great credit, several hundred of them did just that. Even the British press were supportive but sensitive in their coverage, which was extensive. Not for the first or the last time, I was very moved by the breadth and depth of the goodwill that exists for Morgan.

While the public firestorm raged, in the background we worked assiduously to get to the bottom of it all. Christopher finally managed to reach a senior official at the ACO and had a long conversation in French. When he finished the call, Christopher's face was ashen. He didn't really need to explain why. I understood French well enough to get the gist of it.

'They say we haven't paid our bloody bills.' He said gruffly and marched out of the office clutching a bunch of papers.

He came back half an hour later. 'Well, that's that. We're stuffed.'

Apparently there was a small outstanding bill regarding expenses for an ACO technical visit to the factory in 2002. No one in the Morgan accounts office remembered seeing the invoice in question. It was many months old and no reminders or statements had ever been received. It seemed we had been tried, sentenced and guillotined for a crime that we didn't even know we had committed.

More long, desperate phone calls to France followed as we tried to explain, to repair the damage. And to beg, even demand a re-trial. But there was no way back. The officials were apologetic, but the decision was made and no mechanism existed by which it could be changed, even if they wanted to – and by this time I do believe they were beginning to feel that they did.

I asked for an emergency meeting of the Morgan board. My PR hat for Morgan has always overridden everything else and I saw real and serious danger for the company if this story leaked uncontrollably. Unusually, on this occasion we did manage to keep control of the rumour mill.

Perception is one thing, reality all too often quite another. Certainly everyone who knew then or has learned about it since will have an opinion about the real truth of the matter. For my own part, it just didn't ring quite true. The amount concerned was tiny in the context of things and the idea that someone would not simply have called to say there was a problem was hard to take seriously.

No, I smelled a rat. It seemed to me that Richard Stanton's impromptu second-hand Morgan sale in Florida might have been even more damaging than I had at first imagined. And his successful application for not one but two entries at Le Mans for his TVR team added to the growing scepticism. My adventures in international motorsport since then have hardly helped to soften this outlook. But for the moment, this was all academic. It was time to start thinking about the Donington race.

In the workshop, Steve Lawrence and his small team were furiously bashing, cutting, grinding and welding to convert the car's technical presentation to the new set of rules. I completed the lengthy entry documentation with help from Christopher and Mark Aston, the senior director at Morgan Motor Company who was the specialist in all matters relating to international homologation.

Here I should explain a little about the way the racing rules are formulated; I was to live in this nightmare for the next eighteen months or so and several major events in the story have their roots in these complex regulations.

There are several classes in international motor racing. What concern us here are the specific narrow categories that directly relate to the Morgan Works

Team. Both Charles Morgan and Christopher Lawrence were always emphatic that they wanted to race in the sports car class that most directly reflects the cars that any punter can buy from a showroom. We made much of this in our press and PR output and in fact one of our fundamental justifications for being involved was based directly on this concept; if racing was to prove the technical superiority and durability of the Aero 8 production car, we clearly needed to race in a production-based class.

Both the FIA and the ACO base their 'sports car' racing categories on roughly the same philosophy; i.e. the basic car must be closely related to the production model, with major modifications strictly controlled within the rules. Under the FIA regime, the category we are concerned with is FIA GTN, while under the ACO's remit, the class is known as LMGT.

Each authority requires the manufacturer to demonstrate that a minimum number of production cars (the actual number is different in each case, but as a guide, we are talking about a few hundred cars) has been built for customers. This is verified by a range of means, including visits to the factory and inspection of sales documentation. The manufacturer is further required to complete very detailed documentation about the production car: photographs, measurements, weights, componentry – every minute detail of the car is recorded. This process is known as homologation. The authority concerned – either FIA or ACO – then takes a completed version of the homologation and an actual production car fresh from the line and compares the two with pedantic attention to detail.

It is tempting to belittle this whole bureaucratic and technical dance as just another job and paper creation exercise; and certainly, there are elements of that. However, there is a very real and important reason why the dance is played out the way it is. It is done in an attempt to stop people cheating.

As a relatively green newcomer to the whole business, I was rather shocked to find this was true. Surely, it's all about taking part, about gentlemen racers, fair play and all that…? No. Actually, it's about winning, pure and simple. Winning at all costs and by whatever means. The reputational stakes are high and the financial costs virtually obscene. Sponsors pay the bills and they want results. Results means cameras; and in the vast majority of cases the cameras will only feature the leading car or two (the Morgan Works Team was the exception that proves the rule). The authorities know this and so do all the teams involved. So everybody learns the dance. Everybody tries to find new moves around the steps; and the authorities keep coming up with new ways to check. It's all a game. When it suits them – and there are many reasons why it might, most of them directly or indirectly involving money – the authorities 'turn a blind eye' or invoke one of the many discretionary clauses that are buried in the depths of the rules.

This brings me to another aspect of the rules, one that gave us interminable headaches throughout the project. Both sets of regulations – FIA and ACO – were originally written in French, and French that is both technical and bureaucratic. The translation into English produced results that sometimes verged on the esoteric, leaving us pondering and arguing over the precise meaning of a single sentence. In other words, sometimes we were not even clear what the rules were; let alone if we actually complied with them.

I hope all that is clear. To return to the Donington entry, Mark Aston was the person responsible for Morgan Motor Company's dealings with all aspects of vehicle approvals, including, in this instance, the critical FIA Homologation documents that confirmed our eligibility to enter the Donington race under FIA rules. Mark is an extremely knowledgeable man who is adept at working through international bureaucracy nightmares that would leave lesser men begging for therapy. He knew the individuals concerned at the FIA Headquarters in Switzerland. No one could be better qualified for the role.

We were aware of a few small problems in the homologation papers. The major one concerned the carbon fibre hard top that had been developed for the race car. Here is a good example of the rules in operation: the *spirit* of the rules was that you should not have something fitted to the race car that is not fitted to the road car – especially if it would give the race car a specific advantage. In this case, the race workshop played an important secondary role as technical development department for the main Morgan production line. This was another of the very positive reasons for taking on a race programme; new ideas and developments – like a carbon fibre hard top, for example – could be developed in the race shop and within days be incorporated into the production lines next door. This was, in fact, exactly what had happened in this case. A hard-top option was already being offered to customers and several ordered one with their new Aero 8. A prototype had already been built and sold. The first production cars were due off the line within days.

But this brings us to the *letter* of the rules. Everything we were doing was completely above board, but we still had to demonstrate that fact. Mark was in almost constant contact with Geneva as race weekend approached. Finally, it was agreed that we would have to take a production car, fully fitted with a hard top, to the race itself to allow the officials to see the hard top for themselves. So the dance continued.

The homologation nightmare was only one of many obstacles I was working on in the team office. There were logistics to deal with. There were sponsors, guests and fans. A great many people were in touch, knowledgeable and angered by the Le Mans rejection and excited about the forthcoming UK debut of the Morgan Works Team. Of course, we had very little money and I tore my hair out as we tried to make ends meet.

For drivers, I had lined up an interesting combination. Neil Cunningham, the New Zealander who had been so impressive in Richard Thorne's British GT car, would be joined by his occasional team mate, Paula Cooke. I liked the idea of having a woman driver on the team. It added a useful new aspect to our team PR and it had to be good for Morgan's image. I hoped it might even have something of a civilizing effect on the crew; perhaps containing their worst macho excesses. Apart from that, Paula was no slouch behind the wheel and, even more important, her sponsor, Jonathon France, was very supportive. The contribution he brought at that point was relatively small, but it was vital.

Our old friend Martin Short – one of the few real gentlemen in the business – came up trumps, agreeing to lend us his race truck and awning for the paddock at cost, solving most of our logistical problems at one stroke. A fax arrived from Geneva, confirming that, with the proviso of sight of a production hard top at the event, the car's homologation was approved. It seemed that we were in business.

My worries now switched to the technical front. Over in the race workshop, all was far from well. The work seemed to be taking forever to complete, despite Steve and his team working up to 18 hours a day. I couldn't understand it. Steve was always very touchy about these matters – it seemed to me that whenever the race deadline was, the mechanics would always be working right up to the very last minute. Although the car was quite clearly a collection of mechanicals, building a race car seemed to have much more in common with art than with science.

'We'll be bloody ready!' was the most helpful comment I could extract from Steve. He was like his father in many ways; the sparse use of language was one of them.

Race weekend was upon us. On Wednesday, I drove up to the circuit to find the truck and the awning already expertly installed by Martin Short's people. I set up camp in the little office in the truck, made myself known to the race officials, spoke to some media and fans and settled down to await the arrival of the car. I called the factory to check on progress. 'We're running behind,' Steve said. 'See you about 8 p.m.' There was nothing to do but wait. We were scheduled for scrutineering first thing on Thursday morning, but I was still quite relaxed. The factory was only a 90-minute drive away and it was far better for them to complete everything before travelling up to Donington.

It was a pretty unpleasant evening. The paddock was still coming together and I found no one I knew during a walkabout. The on-site catering wasn't open yet, so I passed a very frugal few hours. I knew it was quite a long way from the circuit to anywhere I could find food, so I was stuck there. eight o'clock came and went, followed in due course by nine o'clock… and ten o'clock.

I had quite consciously not called Steve before. But now I did call and after three or four attempts managed to get through. Alarmingly, I heard the familiar screech of grinders and hammering almost drowning out the conversation. It was brief and to the point.

'How is it going, Steve?'

'We've got a few problems.'

'When do you reckon, then?'

'I dunno. Maybe midnight…' He didn't sound convincing.

I waited. It became very cold soon after dark and I huddled in the little truck office, trying to sleep while I could. It was virtually impossible. I saw midnight, then one, two o'clock. There was no point in calling them again.

I lay awake through those strange, mysterious hours between three and five in the morning, worry and doubt growing in my tired, cold mind as each minute dragged impossibly slowly by. Then the sun was up and soon the paddock early risers were up and about, bleary-eyed figures carrying towels and wash bags. At this point, it occurred to me that I would probably have paid £10 for a decent cup of coffee. There was none to be had. It was now approaching six in the morning. I badly needed to hear from the team.

Finally, I heard from them. They were stopped a short distance away at a service station, getting breakfast and coffee.

'Good morning gentlemen,' I said. 'Could you please get here as quickly as possible and for God's sake, bring me a coffee!'

Soon I was down at the gate, watching the battered old Morgan 'Sprinter' van and, behind it, the 'horse box' trailer it towed, containing the precious race car. It was a poignant contrast to the gleaming, million dollar rigs parked up in the paddock around us. I was very, very pleased to see it and them – the grinning, grubby faces, complete with two-day stubble and 'no sleep' eyes that peered out from the cab.

'Morning!' They chanted in unison.

However affectionate we may have felt about the old van and trailer, it was not exactly good for the image. As it was still very early in the morning, I wanted to get the car off and into the paddock tent and the van and trailer parked somewhere well out of sight before the paddock woke up properly. We nearly pulled this off, but unloading the car, with its very low ground clearance, from the 'horsebox', was a complicated piece of alchemy involving various pieces of wood, an old trolley jack, a lot of pushing and pulling and copious cursing. Clearance inside the horsebox was about 2cm each side; some wisecrack made a rude comparison between this and the production tolerances at the factory.

There was simply no way to keep such a show quiet, even at seven in the morning, and a small crowd gathered to watch, their faces showing a strange mixture of amusement, disbelief and pity. Finally it was done. The car was safely under canvas and the team's battered toolboxes and other sundry kit had been unloaded. The van and trailer disappeared to the furthest reaches of Donington Park.

The car did not look good. In fact, it looked as if people had been crawling all over it all night; which was of course precisely true. It was covered in grinding dust and greasy finger and hand marks. We had just a couple of hours to spare before scrutineering, so cleaning and polishing began in earnest. The sun came up shining and the car began slowly to look more presentable.

The same could not be said about the team. Even a change into race day 'best' overalls could not disguise the fact that they had worked all the previous night and most of the one before that, too. They needed a long hot bath – and a few days' rest. As we polished, we had a visitation from one of the minor race officials. He pulled up on his moped and said, rather sneeringly, in a strong German accent, 'You had better hurry up and get to scrutineering. You must not be late. I hear that your car is not even properly homologated.'

We knew who this man was. We also knew that he had very strong connections with the many Porsche teams that comprised the great majority of the GTN class. It was nice to be so warmly welcomed to our first FIA race.

All too soon, it was time to go. I gathered the master file of paper work and we pushed the car down the paddock to scrutineering, the team still trying to polish the car as it rolled along.

Over the years, I have found it useful to develop a keen eye for body language. Combined with a basic understanding of French and German, this knowledge can be a real advantage in any international working environment. I watched and listened carefully as the technical scrutineers began their work. Two things were obvious: they were not particularly happy to see the Morgan; and they were determined to find difficulties. I left Steve Lawrence and Dave Bradley to argue over the size and position of air vents and other fascinating details, while I got on with the paper-based side of registration.

The interview was not dissimilar in tone to the warm and friendly exchanges that were common in Cold War Eastern Europe;

'Good morning, gentlemen,' I put on my best smile and eye contact.

'Papers!' The Official was Very Important. He held the Power to Allow you to Race. He demanded Respect. I handed over the papers.

The Official and a sidekick pored over the documents. I got the distinct impression that they were looking for something in particular and that somehow they knew in advance what they would find.

Finally, The Official fixed me with ice-cold eyes. 'Your car is not homologated,' he said, as if pronouncing a death sentence – which in a way, he was.

I tried to remain calm, polite and respectful. I found the copy of the fax from the FIA's Geneva HQ and pointed out that it said, quite clearly, '…subject to viewing of the production hard top, the race car will be homologated to race at Donington.' The officials examined the fax briefly and then handed it back to me.

'We have not received any confirmation from Geneva that your car is homologated,' said The Official. 'Therefore, it is NOT homologated. I cannot allow you to race.' The absence of the word 'sorry' from this communication spoke volumes.

'I am sure we can solve this easily. Could you please call Geneva?'

A brief phone call was made. The Official translated the outcome, though he did not need to do so – my schoolboy French was again up to the job. The person who had sent the fax to us, the person who could overrule this Official and confirm our eligibility, had gone away on holiday.

I felt an icy blast in my insides.

Back outside, I met up with Steve and Dave. 'We have a few problems…' began Bradders. 'I'm afraid we have one very big one,' I interrupted. I quickly shared with them the highlights of the meeting. Back in the little office in the truck, I desperately tried to think clearly, to establish some kind of logical action plan. I called Mark Aston, the first of hundreds of phone calls I was to make that day. In Mark's voice, I could hear the beginnings of a quite understandable fear; as the person responsible for homologation, his own neck was very exposed. He promised to call everyone he could think of in Geneva, including trying to get a mobile number for the senior official who was now on holiday. Mark would also be able to appraise Charles and the other Morgan directors of the situation as soon as he arrived at the factory. The latter comment brought me back to the real world with a jolt. I looked at my watch; it was still not even nine o'clock in the morning.

My next call was to Christopher. Ever the calm, unflappable pragmatist, he listened carefully to the story before simply saying, 'Well, you're doing everything that can be done. That's all we can ask. Good luck.'

For the moment, the ball was with Mark Aston. At the circuit, things began to happen very quickly as the morning got fully under way. Jonathon France, our new and supportive sponsor, arrived with Paula Cooke and I took them both aside to explain the position we were in. They both received the very unwelcome news calmly. I assured them that we would not admit defeat until every possible stone had been turned. Neil Cunningham arrived shortly afterwards and I repeated the sad tale to him, too.

I gathered Steve and the team around and explained where we were. It was important to try to keep a calm grip. I asked Steve for an overview of the technical scrutineering. There were a few jobs to do, mostly filling in air vents that the officials had taken a dislike to. Nothing major. However, there was another paper issue. Apparently the certificate of authenticity for our safety roll cage was a fax copy, not the original. Some beady-eyed official had spotted this and was apparently prepared to forbid us from racing unless the original document was produced in time. I began to have a sneaking feeling that someone, somewhere, for some reason or another, did not want the Morgan to take part in this race.

The following hour or so is a blur in my memory. My phone must have glowed hot, as call followed call in an unbroken stream. The roll cage supplier was based in Devon; several hundred miles away. Somehow we needed to persuade him to produce a certified copy of the documentation and get it to us at the circuit within a few short hours. Mark Aston was being sent in circles around the FIA organisation, but it was becoming clear that we were unlikely to get hold of the one person who could help. He was apparently on a transatlantic flight and would not be contactable for several hours. We were completely snookered in that direction. Christopher and Charles had been talking to every one of their many high level official contacts on the UK motorsports scene. People were very sympathetic and understanding, but there was little that they could do of practical help. Senior British officials called senior FIA officials. The FIA would simply not be moved.

Time was running out. I spoke once more with Christopher and Charles. We agreed that it was worth one more shot; I would have to go to the senior race officials and try a personal appeal.

I waited in the outer room until the all-powerful were ready to receive me. Eventually, I was ushered in and directed to a single seat. Across a large, empty desk sat three officials. Eventually, they acknowledged my existence. 'Ah, Morgan. Yes?'

Trying to keep my voice calm and my attitude suitably respectful, I summarised our predicament, presenting it as an unfortunate breakdown in communication. It was perfectly clear from our fax documentation that FIA HQ was completely satisfied with our homologation papers. We had arranged the production car for viewing as requested. The original roll cage document was en route as we spoke. Many fans were coming to see the Morgan run… The officials listened politely until I had finished my piece. There was no discussion between them. The boss spoke quietly; 'I am sorry, Mr Dowse. We have not received confirmation from Geneva that your car has been homologated. Therefore it is *not* homologated. We cannot allow you to take part in the race. Thank you and good morning.' I was being dismissed.

I was still determined to keep trying. 'Please, gentlemen,' I said. They looked quite shocked that I had the gall to speak further. 'For the sake of the fans who have travelled here especially to see the Morgan; could you not let us start the race from the back of the grid? Or even take part in practice and not race, so the fans can at least see the car? '

'I am afraid that is not possible, Mr Dowse.'

'Well, then, just a couple of demonstration laps during lunch or something?'

This was desperation. I knew it. And so did they.

'So there's nothing we can do, except pack up and go home?' I finished, anger and frustration finally cracking in my voice.

'We'll see you next time, Mr Dowse. Goodbye.'

I didn't go straight back to the camp. Instead, I found a coffee bar and sat quietly. There was nothing more to be done. What mattered now was how we played it. I informed the team first. For them, it meant an early bath, a good meal and an easy day 'on holiday' at the races. Small enough compensation for the disappointment of working all hours for weeks on end to finish the car only to have it banished from the race because of a stupid bureaucratic cock-up; but compensation, nonetheless.

I decided that we would leave the car on display in the paddock for the rest of the weekend, rather than pack up and go home. In fact, the cut and run option was quite attractive to me personally, but by now I had switched into PR mode and I had a plan, or at least, half of one.

I wrote a brief, terse statement for the press, explaining exactly why the Morgan would not be running that weekend and specifically, the apparent breakdown of communications between two departments of the FIA that meant we had to sit out the weekend in the paddock. It did not take long to have its effect. Within half an hour of posting the release in the media centre, one of the younger, friendlier FIA officials visited the Morgan tent, clutching a copy.

'David, this isn't going to help you, you know.' He said quietly.

'Maybe not, but it sure as hell makes me feel better.' I replied.

'They won't like it...' 'They' were the senior FIA people, of course. I was being told that I shouldn't criticise them. Well, personally, I had had my fill of eating humble pie for one weekend.

'Maybe. But I don't like it much, either. We've worked our butts off to get here. You've taken our money for the entry and we've spent a small fortune – in our terms, anyway, getting here. Now they won't let us race because of some paperwork crap. It's shit. So if they don't like it, that's too bad. I am not going to be censored by anybody.'

It was good to let off steam, even if the poor chap who received the blast was not responsible.

It was still only ten thirty in the morning. Crowds were beginning to gather. Natasha arrived and I filled her in with the sorry tale. As ever, she responded brilliantly and soon we were both caught up with talking with large crowds of well-wishers and fans flocking to the barriers at the front of the Morgan tent, wanting to know why the car wasn't out on the circuit for free practice. The media started to come by, too, and now the recovery plan started to come to fruition.

Somewhere in the dim and distant past, my PR training had included a lesson about 'finding a silver lining' in the darkest cloud. The early part of that morning had seemed not so much like the inside of a dark cloud, but more like the end of all light and hope. Coming so soon after the Le Mans entry shock, this was surely the very worst outcome imaginable. How would we persuade sponsors to work with us now? How could we build a fan base when the car wasn't even running? How could we even find the willpower to carry on? These and many other impossible questions had raced through my mind during the 'coffee break' earlier. But there had to be a silver lining, a positive line...

The answer had dawned on me as I was walking back to the camp from the coffee bar. If we played this right, it could actually help to build the Morgan legend. But the message needed to be bang on. I briefed Natasha and we set to work.

We played down the paper work issue, leaving the British fans and the British media, with the vague feeling that it had something to do with European bureaucracy. They could very easily relate to that.

'It's such a shame,' we said over and over again. 'We were ready to roll. Makes you wonder what those Porsches are afraid of, doesn't it?' This last was said in a very tongue-in-cheek manner, but it was a powerful message and the fans loved it.

By the middle of the afternoon, both Natasha and I had virtually lost our voices. It had been one hell of a day. We deserved a drink and back at the team hotel, we got one. As the wine flowed, so did the conspiracy theories. The more we thought it through, the more it seemed that someone had decided well before the race that the Morgan would not be welcome at the Donington race. Why on earth should that be? OK, we were an unknown factor, but surely, after the car's less than scintillating performances during the 2002 campaign, nobody could seriously feel threatened by it? Unless our PR was having even more of an effect than we thought… no, it didn't add up. But then there was the guy on the moped. He *knew* we had a problem, all right. It was a long night.

Race day was more of the same, with the added complications of corporate guests and sponsors arriving – those whom we had not been able to contact in time to prevent them travelling. Our 'victim of bureaucracy' line held up well and it seemed that everyone was sympathetic.

As we packed up, I was almost persuaded that we had made a very good impact. And there was little doubt in my mind that personally, I had learned and grown through the fire of experience.

nine

A star in the car

Back at the factory, it was quickly decided that we must go on. The Spa 24 Hour race was only a few weeks away. Nobody was in any doubt that this really was our last chance to redeem ourselves. This time, there must be no room for doubt.

Deciding what to do is one thing. Making it happen is quite another. The disastrous outing to Donington, just up the road from Malvern, had still eaten up over £20,000 in operational costs; and that was after much begging and borrowing and calling in of favours. Taking the whole operation to a 24-hour race in Belgium was going to need a lot more cash. On the day we decided to go, we had no idea where it was going to come from.

The fall out from Donington was not too bad, though it was a little annoying to see just how easily the homologation problem was solved once the Geneva-based official was back from playing golf. There was no apology.

The media coverage was generally sympathetic and the few technical sponsors who had stayed with us after the Le Mans entry shock continued to be supportive. But finding any new sponsorship was proving to be extremely difficult. I spent many hours on the phone, writing proposals and giving presentations. Many people were very friendly and sympathetic, but nobody was prepared to bring out the chequebook. 'If you get to Le Mans next year, please do talk to us...' was a common response. I tried to point out that if we didn't get some support soon, we were extremely unlikely ever to get to Le Mans again, but there was little future in that line of argument.

I could see it from the sponsor's point of view – at least to a degree. On one level, the Morgan Works Team was small and insignificant. Even the most optimistic among us did not expect the car to actually *win* – unless an act of God resulted in the mass early retirement of all the Porsches. So far, the Aero 8 had not even completed a race properly, let alone made an impression. So the standard motorsport formula clearly appeared to apply: unless you're winning, you don't attract media; and if you don't attract media, you don't attract sponsors.

The problem was that in the case of the Morgan Team, the perceived wisdom was simply wrong. What the potential sponsors failed to grasp – or I suppose one might fairly say, what I failed to persuade them of – was that in this case, there was a unique opportunity for someone to achieve enormous exposure, for relatively little investment. And it was possible precisely *because* this was Morgan; precisely *because* we did not have a hope of winning.

From the outset, I saw the Morgan Le Mans campaign as a unique, one time only exercise. Whatever it was that I had witnessed in the pits in 2002 was very special and certainly it had moved and inspired me – and others – to take on the impossible. Of course, it is very difficult to define. It was about big-hearted spirit, about taking on the impossible, about having a go against all the odds. Self-belief, courage, creativity. Sheer, bloody-minded determination – and the total refusal to accept defeat; these are some of the qualities that I believe defined the Morgan Way.

That's all very laudable. But leaving aside for a moment those rare, wonderful individuals who are both wealthy enough and adventurous enough to want to support such madness, commercially driven sponsors need more. Much more. They need the oxygen of publicity, their logo on camera in return for their money.

This is where I part ways with the logic and understanding of so many marketing people. My point was simple; if the PR was managed correctly (and we had already shown that we were extremely effective) the Morgan story could light up the world's imagination in a way that only the very largest of the other teams could manage. It did not matter one jot if we ran the whole race at the back of the field; the cameras would be on Morgan because Morgan was Morgan.

In straightforward commercial terms, this meant that the right sponsor could achieve fantastic results for relatively little money; and what's more, because of our desperate plight, we could offer headline sponsorship for around the same investment as one of the front running teams would provide an insignificant sticker. How could they refuse?

Despite my evangelism and despite the inescapable logic of the argument, refuse they did.

Neil Cunningham was a powerhouse of energy, both on the circuit and off. He never rested from hustling, cajoling and persuading. His valiant efforts delivered various small but important bonuses; in particular, his introduction to Colin North at Teng Tools led to a very kind donation from Colin of all the tools the team needed but had never had before. We were extremely grateful for his support.

In his own, very different way, Charles Morgan was also trying to find supporters and it was he who saved the day on this occasion. Prince E. Sturzda, a wealthy Swiss banker and an enthusiastic Morgan fan, was also a close personal friend of Jacques Lafitte, the famous French Formula One driver. They visited the Morgan factory together and over lunch at a local pub, a deal was struck. I knew nothing about this until Charles walked into the little office and asked, 'How would you like to have Jacques Lafitte in the car at Spa?'

It was a fantastic morale boost and there was also a very helpful sponsorship package attached from Banque Barings Bros (Suisse). At last, here was a forward-looking, visionary company that understood what an association with the Morgan brand could do for them.

Delighted and relieved in equal measure, I issued a press release confirming a very exciting driver line up – Jacques Lafitte, Neil Cunningham and Paula Cooke. Paula's sponsor, Jonathon France, had been very understanding about the Donington debacle and still very much wanted Paula to drive with us. He was quite excited about the prospect of sharing the honours with Jacques Lafitte and Neil was absolutely over the moon when I broke the news to him. Paula herself was strangely cool about it, though.

With a budget to work with, I could now get on with the complex logistics of getting the team, the car and equipment to the race and also to dealing with the VIP guests that would inevitably come attached to the kind support Prince Sturzda was providing.

The logistical nightmare was further complicated by our need to get some proper testing under our belts before starting a 24-hour race. Through the good auspices of Morgan's unique relationship with BMW, we were able to use the German company's superb testing facilities at Miramas in the South of France. All we had to do was get the car, our equipment and a small team of specialist mechanics down there.

But before we went, we also needed to get the car on to a suspension analysis rig; and the one chosen was in Norfolk.

As ever, time was crushing down on us and solving it all was rather like playing three-dimensional chess. To give the reader a better understanding of what was involved, it is perhaps worth a little more detailed explanation.

The car itself travelled in the old horsebox trailer, pulled by the Sprinter van, which was loaded to capacity with essential kit for running the car both at testing in Miramas and then at the race itself. This rig was to be driven by my bother-in-law, Tim Fitzgerald, who was about to embark on an epic journey across Europe.

Stage one was relatively simple; the van and trailer were loaded up at the factory and left around midnight for the long drive down to Norfolk. I followed in my car, along with Steve Lawrence, Dave Bradley and Rogier Vancamelbecke. These three now formed the core technical team. We soon caught up and overtook the van and trailer and I was alarmed as I saw how heavily loaded the rig was. Poor Tim. He was in for a very long, slow drive, with the very real danger that the trailer would blow a tyre or that the ancient suspension would finally give up the ghost.

Four hours later, we arrived at the hotel just as the light began to touch the eastern sky. We were all asleep seconds after our heads hit the pillow. Tim rolled in a couple of hours behind us.

We had 4 hours' sleep, followed by a good breakfast. I left Tim to sleep in; he had done his bit for the moment and he had another very long drive ahead that night. One of the others drove the rig and soon we were installed at the suspension test facility. Known as a 'four-poster' the test bed is a highly complex machine. Data sensors are fitted all over the car's suspension and it is then subjected to a long series of tests. The results are all gathered together and analysed by computer; ultimately giving a highly detailed picture of how the suspension and chassis are working and, in theory, suggesting any improvements or changes that might improve performance.

It was a long process. I left them to it and returned to the hotel to spend an hour or so on the 'phone. Tim joined me for lunch and we went over the rest of the logistics plan together.

When the tests were finished, Tim was to pick up the car and then head for Dover. He would drive down through France, stopping somewhere en route to sleep. If all went well, he should arrive in Miramas the following evening, where he was to find the hotel, park up and await the arrival of the team. I would take the team back to Malvern, where they would help load up the secondary truck the following morning before heading off to the airport for a flight down to Miramas.

The advance team, who would fit out the pits at Spa, would travel down to Belgium in the 7-ton truck, loaded with all the pit equipment. I would follow down in my car.

The Miramas team would do two days of testing before packing up the van and trailer. The mechanics would then fly up to Spa, while the long-suffering Tim would drive back up through Europe to deliver the car and the rest of the kit to the circuit.

If all this sounds over-complicated, it is because we were juggling a huge number of requirements. We had to fit in with available time on the test circuit and of course be ready for scrutineering, practice and qualifying at the circuit. It was not reasonable to expect the technical team to successfully run a 24-hour race directly after driving through the night in an uncomfortable minibus; hence some of the complication was about trying to allow people as much sleep and rest as was feasible.

Remarkably, the convoluted plan worked smoothly. I arrived on site in good time to supervise the setting up of our catering operations and the motor home that would serve as my hotel room, the team office and driver rest area. Having a serious sponsor and a VIP guest driver meant that we had to make as good an impression as possible. I was very much hoping to show Prince Sturzda that, given funding, I could deliver a top quality result. So here at Spa, for the first time, we had 'proper' catering facilities and a large, comfortable motor home. For once, we did not feel like a bunch of down and outs.

Our pit garage was located up at the top of the hill, a little away from the cramped paddock area down by the grandstands and this suited us quite well. Certainly we had more space. As we did not own a big race truck with an awning, like everyone else did, I had come up with a plan that involved a large, hired tented structure built on to the back of our pit garage. This would house all the spares and our 'backstage' working area.

Everything was coming together. We had brought our own materials to build a substantial lighting rig inside the pits and out front and I had spent a little precious money on pit decoration boards too. Unable to afford the special plastic flooring that everyone uses, we had brought some industrial carpet – this would be thrown away after the race, but newly laid and clean, it made our garage look pretty.

By the end of our second day on site, all was prepared. The news from Miramas was good; the testing had gone well, the team had made their flight on time and Tim was well under way on his long haul up through Europe. He had a lot of responsibility on him; it was crucial that he arrived at Spa first thing in the morning. Any later and it would soon become virtually impossible to get into the site with the trailer. He would have to drive solidly, all night, without major stops. 'Whatever you do, don't breakdown or get lost!' My final words to him at around two in the morning were probably not helpful.

At a quarter past six the following morning, I was awoken by my mobile phone. 'I'm at the gate. Is the kettle on?' He had made it, bless him. 'You're a star!' I said and I meant it.

We put the car into the prepared pit garage and put Tim to bed in the motor home.

The van and the trailer were again hidden somewhere off at the circuit's edge so that they did not let down the carefully constructed image.

While the team set to work polishing and making final preparations for scrutineering, I went back to the motor home. While Tim slept the sleep of the innocent in the bedroom area, I went over the master file of documentation once again. The nightmare of Donington was painfully fresh in my mind and I knew that neither the team, nor me personally, would be likely to survive another episode like that. The papers were perfect, so far as I could tell. We would not have to wait very much longer to find out.

Body and spoken language antennas fully active, I went into scrutineering with the others. Faces that were familiar from Donington met us, but somehow, there was a milder aspect to them this time. Again, I left Steve and Bradders with the technical processes and went into the lion's den of administrative sign-on. I handed over the documents. They were examined. They were handed back, without comment, along with the signed passport to enter the race. Subject to technical scrutineering, we were in.

For the benefit of readers who may not be familiar with the details of this ritual, I should like to take a few moments to explain what goes on. I hope those who do know will forgive me.

Scrutineering is designed to ensure that the car is safe to race and meets the technical requirements of the rules; that is, nothing has been done to the car that might give it an advantage. This is the official line.

In reality, though, I have come to think that scrutineering is actually designed to give the scrutineers a reason to be important; and crucially, to be important visibly, so that the world *knows* they are important. They have real power. Remember, one of these individuals can ultimately stop you from racing. No matter that you have worked for months to get there, that you have mortgaged your house and probably your soul, that the jobs and well being of many innocents may depend on it. They are without mercy. Thankfully, they rarely do this; though it does happen. More often, they will simply enjoy knowing that you know they have the power if they chose to use it.

The sadism of the scrutineers can be breathtaking. One of their favourite pleasures is to give the team many hours of completely pointless work to do, against the clock and in the difficult environment of a pit garage. The sentences of torture they hand down can often keep the team working all night – preferably the night before a 24-hour endurance race. I am convinced that this is often done in the well-established European tradition '…*pour encourager les autres.*'

Thankfully, the list of work was not extensive this time. Perhaps the scrutineers remembered our suffering at Donington and took pity on us. I doubt it. In any case, after messing about taking the seat and fuel cell out so that they could read the numbers on the respective labels, we had passed. This time, Cinderella would go to the ball.

Words cannot convey the sense of utter relief I felt that evening. I called Christopher and Charles to let them know we were cleared to race. Tomorrow, Jacques Lafitte and the other drivers would arrive and after lunch the first free practice session would finally see the Morgan back on the racetrack again. It had been a long wait. Sitting alone in the motor home after everyone had gone back to their hotels, I reviewed everything that had happened before sleeping as only the reprieved can sleep.

I am not sure what time the rain started. As I pulled back the curtains in the motor home and peered outside, all I could see was a grey, wet shroud covering the surrounding hillsides. It had the look of many mountainous areas; it would be easy to imagine that it had been raining forever and would rain forever more.

Situated as it is in beautiful, pine-clad hills, the Spa circuit has a reputation for wet races – so much so that older and wiser advisors had told me that it would be extremely unusual to escape at least one or two downpours during a 24-hour race weekend.

I had fresh coffee, orange juice and croissants in the little motor home kitchen and was soon joined by a smiling Neil Cunningham. It was still only around eight o'clock but typically, Neil's unbounded enthusiasm had him at the circuit and raring to go; hours before any action was scheduled. We talked in depth about the programme and where we hoped it was going. In his usual kind fashion, Neil was very encouraging. 'You've done a great job getting us this far, mate,' he said in his wonderful accent – a unique and beguiling mixture of the New Zealand of his birth, the Australia where he grew up and the Wales which was now his home. 'I reckon it's been bloody hard going…'

Neil knew the business very well indeed and he had been closely involved throughout the most intimate trails and tribulations of the team – always supportive and always suggesting solutions. I have never met anyone more positive about life; and his almost total lack of ego made his company even more endearing.

'Neil, I'm not even sure why I'm doing this,' I replied. 'I just want to get Morgan back to Le Mans and finish what we started.'

'Well, we're here and I reckon if we can do well, we'll be on our way, mate.' Just looking at him, I could see he was desperate to get behind the wheel of the car.

Miraculously, the rain had stopped and the sun was threatening to shine. I left Neil watching re-runs of old races on the video in the motor home and went off to check on the Morgan camp at the top of the hill. I was very pleased with the presentation. The catering looked top notch; leaving me relaxed about the imminent arrival of Jacques Lafitte and our VIP sponsor guests.

A short distance way, the pit garage and backroom set-up was also looking good. The car was installed under its lights and the team was working in a relatively relaxed fashion on the list of small technical issues that had arisen from scrutineering. Morale was good and the banter flew thick and fast.

I sat down with Dave Bradley and Steve Lawrence for a coffee and a quick catch-up on the Miramas tests.

'Well, apart from Paula nearly piling the car into a wall on the first day, it went pretty well,' said Bradders. Paula was a relatively unknown quantity and I was a little disturbed to hear this news. She had not responded to strict instructions from the team and had raced off, apparently trying to prove something – taking silly, unnecessary risks in an attempt to beat Neil's lap times. This was not professional behaviour and it threatened the whole project. I knew I would have to have a talk with Jonathon France as soon as he arrived.

Bradders also quietly told me about an intermittent engine electronics issue that had proved impossible to track down, even using the extremely advanced data analysis equipment installed in the car.

'It's really weird,' he said. 'We're getting this very occasional cut-out, which we've not been able to replicate. I've replaced all the wiring looms that could possibly be relevant and we can't see any logic in the cut-outs at all.' I didn't like the sound of this much. 'So how do we handle it?' I asked. 'I've put in a quick re-boot procedure – so if it happens, the driver can just start her up again in a couple of seconds. I've tested it and it works every time. It's all I can do.'

Our conversation was interrupted by the arrival of Jonathon and I broke off to show him around the camp and have the quiet chat we needed about Paula's attitude. He was quite understanding. 'OK, David, I'll have a talk with her – she's usually pretty good with this kind of thing.'

Back at catering, a sudden flurry of activity marked the arrival of Jacque Lafitte's entourage. It was quite a large party, which included Jacques himself, his delightful 'manager', Philippe Rollet ('Actually, I am Jacque's mother!'), Prince Eric Sturzda, the sponsor who had made both the race and Jacque's involvement in it possible, one or two children – nieces of either Jacques or Prince Sturzda – and a small dog.

During my working life, I have had the privilege of meeting several more or less 'famous' wealthy people. Some have appeared to be quite reasonable, sane people; but sadly, many others have proved to be victims of ego who have virtually lost the ability to be human.

Sitting around the little table in our catering tent, I realised that here were individuals who inhabited a world of wealth, privilege and international fame. Within a few minutes of small talk, I was really delighted to find that they were also truly human, warm and open people. Despite their elite positions, they appeared to expect nothing and were genuinely grateful for the hospitality we were able to offer them. I particularly noticed how well they treated the catering staff serving them and, of course, consequently how easily the VIPs won the hearts of everyone they touched. Coming so soon after the equally warm breakfast with Neil, this brief liaison further lifted my spirits and renewed my sagging faith in humanity. It was turning into quite a good day.

I took Jacques over to the pits to see the car and meet the team. His warm and friendly manner immediately extended to every one of the mechanics; he

Steve Lawrence shows Jacques Lafitte over the Aero 8. (DailySportsCar.com)

made a point of meeting and greeting each one, from the senior technicians to the lowliest tyre washer. And once again, it was clear to see that within a few seconds, Jacques had them eating out of his hand; I knew that they would move mountains for him. Leaving Jacques to familiarise himself with the idiosyncrasies of the team and the car, I chatted briefly to Prince Sturzda. He quickly insisted that I address him simply as 'Eric' and demonstrated a wonderful ability to make me feel like a trusted and valued friend. He declared himself delighted with the branding I had arranged for his company, 'Barings Bros Banque' and with all the other arrangements.

During many previous training sessions, I had first learned myself and then subsequently tried to teach others, how important good management communications are – and how very simple it can be to get it right. Eric and Jacques had been with us for less than an hour, but through their natural humanity and by directly *connecting* with everyone on the team – from the team manager to the catering staff and the tyre washers, they had won us all over. Nothing rewards like thanks and praise and the feeling that one is genuinely valued. And nothing costs less to deliver.

Soon it was time for some action. The track was opened for free practice and Neil took the car out for a few shakedown laps. Everything went well and soon Jacques was in the car, his whole attitude so relaxed that he might have been off for a Sunday afternoon drive in the park. I swear, if the driver's window had opened fully, he would have had his elbow out on the sill. 'We'll fit a stereo system for you tomorrow, Jacques!' quipped one of the team over the radio set as Jacques was being strapped in. Two thumbs up from Jacques illustrated his approval of this idea and the situation in general. He was thoroughly enjoying himself.

A demonstration of consummate professionalism followed. Jacque's first couple of laps were very slow compared with the other cars on the track. But then, as his familiarity with the car and the circuit grew, he began to knock two seconds off each consecutive lap. Soon, he was circulating well within the target band. He came into the pits and handed over to Paula, somehow making the act seem like he was a gentleman throwing down his coat over a puddle for her to walk on.

The first session was quickly over, with everyone pronouncing themselves happy. I asked Jacques if he would like to get some more time in the car during the afternoon session. '*Mais, non!*' he grinned. 'That is enough of cars for today. This afternoon, I will go to play golf!' I offered them a lift to the car park on our golf buggy – an essential tool for getting around the large, steeply hilled circuit. Jacques accepted gratefully, then insisted on driving the buggy himself, to the obvious delight of the large and growing crowds in the paddock, who surrounded the buggy, demanding autographs and handshakes from the great French driver.

The rest of the day was uneventful and the second practice session went off without any sign of the engine cut-out problem. Buoyed by the car's

Jacques Lafitte in stylish action on track at Spa. (Melissa Warren)

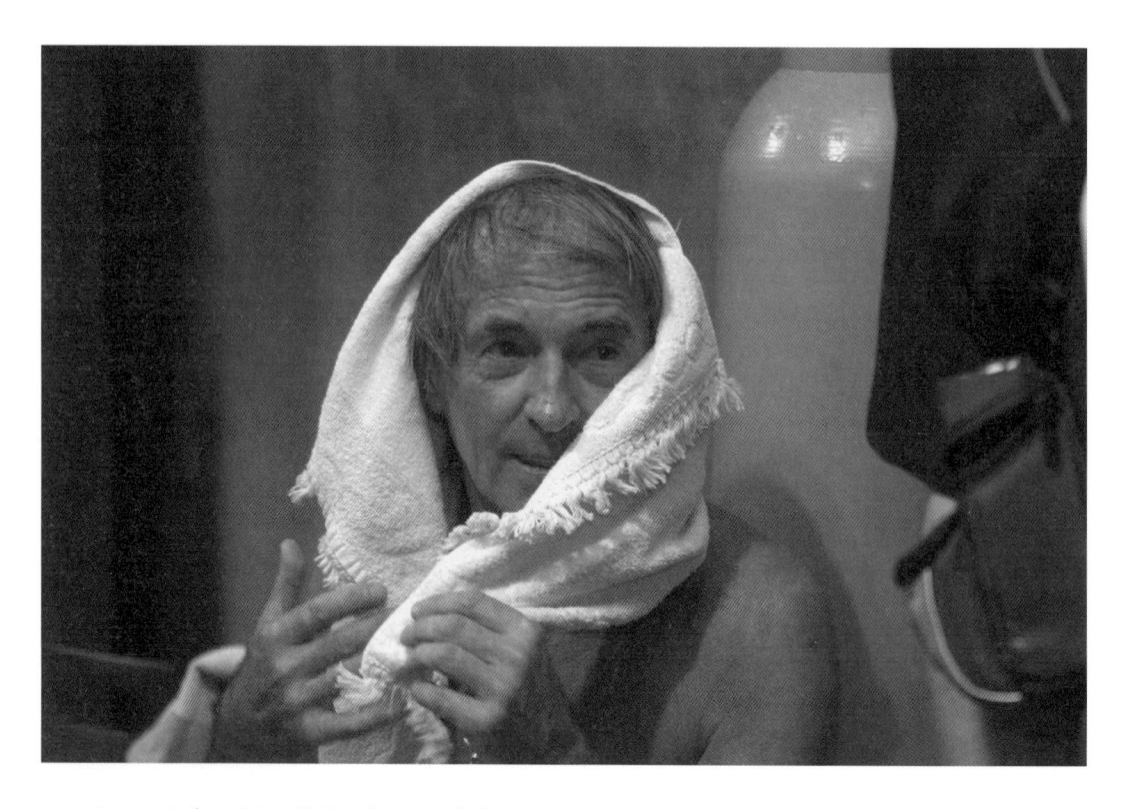

Jacques Lafitte dries off after showing all the others how its done. (Melissa Warren)

performance and glowing from the visitation from Jacques, the team was in high spirits as we all gathered together at catering for the evening meal. The difference from the shock and depression of Donington, just a few short weeks before, was very noticeable and I went to an early bed happy and hopeful that at last, we had turned a corner.

During the night it rained hard again, and the forecast predicted that more rain was virtually certain during the race weekend. Today was to be qualifying and it seemed quite likely that at least some of it would take place in wet conditions. This could be interesting; though we had never had the opportunity to run the race car in the wet, Christopher was quite adamant that the Aero 8's unique suspension geometry meant it would perform very well in the wet. We would not have to wait long to find out if this was so.

Paula nailed the best qualifying time to the scoreboard, much to Neil's chagrin; it was clear that the needle match that had started in France was still very much alive. I tried to calm everyone down, reminding them that the idea was to qualify with the car and all three drivers still in one piece – there were parts of the Spa circuit that could easily end our race ambitions if there was even the smallest lapse in concentration or unnecessary chances were taken. I am quite sure that my words had little or no effect. Drivers are drivers because they simply have to go as fast as the conditions will allow. It takes great maturity to control this instinct.

During the qualifying sessions, I had the opportunity to watch the team in race action. I already knew from watching what had gone on at Le Mans in 2002 just how critical are the dynamics between people. If there are any cracks, any weaknesses, the intense pressure of a race situation will quickly find them. We had already been through many changes of personnel and over time we would need to forge a team that could hack it. So I watched. After a short time in the pits, I had reached a clear conclusion about two individuals. One of them was going to be relatively easy to deal with; the other would be rather more tricky and I would have to wait for the appropriate time.

The rain came down heavily during Jacques' first qualifying drive and almost immediately he reported an engine cut out. 'Both engine switches to completely off, then back on again, Jacques,' Bradders instructed over the radio. This was the agreed emergency procedure. Dave's eyes locked with mine across the garage for a second. Jacques quickly reported he was under way again.

More phone conversations to Heini Mader's office in Switzerland followed later that afternoon in a desperate attempt to track down the elusive engine problem. It was proving a very tough nut to crack. Finally, it was agreed that a new engine would be fitted the night before the race.

Charles Morgan arrived at the circuit and was quickly enjoying the company of Jacques, Eric and their entourage. Later, a very senior representative from Mecachrome, the large French engine company arrived and was in deep conversation with Charles for some time. It seemed that Mecachrome was at an advanced stage of negotiations to buy out the Mader operation, with potentially significant long-term implications for Morgan's race programme. I took Charles aside and appraised him about the engine difficulties; the timing seemed strangely appropriate.

There was now a constant stream of fans arriving at the catering tent to see Jacques – some were, or at least claimed to be, old friends of his, others were simply punters, well-wishers and collectors of autographs. Natasha and I spent several hours on duty at the entrance to the tent, doing our best to manage the demand and keep everyone happy. Many Morgan fans had arrived too and the tent was packed all afternoon.

Later, the car was shipped down into the town centre of Spa to take part in various PR activities along with the other teams. With the Aero 8 safely parked up in its compound, there was a rare break in work and we all gathered for a few welcome cold beers in a café overlooking the scene. Steve Lawrence complained about not being allowed to join the rest of us, but he was down to drive the car back to the circuit as part of a cavalcade arranged by the race organisers to drum up more local interest.

The team hard at work preparing for the overnight engine change at Spa. (DailySportsCar.com)

Selected race cars from each class would drive the 10km or so along public roads back to the circuit – making quite a spectacle, even though their speed was supposed to be strictly limited. Once we had installed Steve in the driver's seat, we jumped in the minibus and drove off to find a good vantage point from which to cheer and jeer as Steve drove past in the Morgan. It was all over in a flash and we headed back to the circuit to bed the car down, quickly followed by ourselves. Tomorrow would be a long hard day.

The team spent the morning removing the engine from the car and getting prepared for the install. The new engine finally arrived in the late afternoon and the team immediately got to work on the complex and difficult job of installing it. 'How long, Steve?' I asked him as dusk began to settle. Tomorrow was race day; looking down the line of garages, ours was the only one with its lights still glowing. 'If it goes alright, should be about 6 hours. We might get to bed by midnight.'

Having made sure they had everything they needed, I knew that it was best to leave them to it. Sending everyone but the essential technical team back to their hotels, I retired to the nearby motor home. 'Call me if you need anything.'

I heard nothing, so I went back towards midnight. They were a long way from being finished and nerves were fraying. There was nothing I could do to help, so I went to bed, feeling guilty but knowing that they would rather not have me hanging around. We had a 0630 start scheduled.

I arrived at the pit garage at 0615. There was no sign of the team. The garage door was firmly locked. Pinned to the outside of it was a big, hand-written sign. 'Please do not feed the animals.' I sat down to wait. Around 20 minutes later, I saw the five of them walking in a line up the hill from the direction of their hotel, looking for all the world like refugees from a spaghetti western.

'Morning,' I greeted them. 'And what time did you finish, gentlemen?' 'About 0430.' So they had had a maximum of 1 hour's sleep, followed by a shower and here they were reporting for duty on race day, with 8 hours of preparation work ahead, followed by a 24-hour race. Not for the first time, I wondered just what these people were made from. They were very far from being ordinary.

The engine install had been very difficult, it appeared; the cramped design of the Aero 8's engine compartment meant that there was very little space to access fixings. Some of the procedures involved looked more like brain surgery than mechanics. But the engine was in, it fired up easily and Neil took the car out on schedule for the early morning warm-up session.

Preparations for the race continued. We agreed that Jacques would start the race, followed by Neil and then Paula. Deciding driver strategy is always very tricky; there are a great many factors that have to be taken into account – the weather, the light conditions and competitor conditions have to be carefully weighed against egos, paying drivers' requirements and contracted minimums and the race regulations concerning maximum driver hours and rest periods.

Finally, everything was set. I wished Jacques the best of luck and went off to find a good vantage point from where I could watch the start.

Our humble qualifying time had placed us quite near to the back of the grid, but in a long-distance race this is no great disadvantage and there is the added bonus that starting from the back the car would be likely to miss the potentially dangerous bunching as the leading cars piled into the first bend.

From the roof of a friendly team's truck, I had a perfect view of the Aero 8 as it sat waiting for the off. After what seemed an age, the track was cleared and engines started. With a massive roar, the cars were off on the formation warm-up lap. The race would begin with a flying start as the front-runners came round for the first time and the lights went green.

As they came up to the start, the roar reached a crescendo and then it was go! What happened next is firmly fixed in my memory. Jacques Lafitte and the Aero 8 seemed to catapult through the field as the cars raced down the pit straight. He effortlessly overtook several cars, weaving through the crowded field before disappearing up the steep hill and into the first right-hander. It was an amazing demonstration of sheer, superior driving skill.

I raced back to the pit garage. 'Did you see that start?' I asked nobody in particular. 'It was really incredible.' Sadly, they had not seen it; as usual, the TV monitors were fixed like glue on the race leaders, so had not captured the amazing action further back.

The team's view of a race from the pits is quite strange. The car goes past every few minutes and there's a fleeting view to be had from the wall as it screams past the pit perch. Apart from that, the team's attention is mostly fixed to two screens; one showing the all important lap speeds and other race data, while the other TV monitor displays shots from around the circuit. It is a very artificial environment. If the pit to car radio system isn't working well – as is all too often the case – you can feel very detached from what's actually happening out there on the track.

We had called dry tyres for the start, but before too long the rain started in earnest and Jacques was back in for a quick tyre change to wets. He was in great spirits, clearly enjoying himself. He even found time during the tyre change to point out the 'glamour' photo that one of the team had fixed to the dashboard, 'To help keep Jacques awake...' The familiar thumbs up and smiling eyes from behind the visor showed his evident appreciation.

He finished a superbly solid first session in appalling conditions, then handed over to Neil, who would take on the tough job of the dusk session as the rain continued to pour down. Soon after he left the pits to begin his session, the weather got so bad that I kept a very close eye on the information screens, expecting the race authorities to stop the race at any moment. The rain was absolutely torrential, bouncing back almost a meter above the track surface. The spray, especially from the faster prototype cars, was impenetrable, reducing visibility to close to zero in places. The cameras flicked around the circuit, showing water pouring in torrents down the steep hills on the circuit. It was a dangerous situation.

Torrential rain brings everyone in for wet tyres. (Melissa Warren)

Neil gets aboard as the weather worsens. Note the absence of wipers. (Melissa Warren)

The Morgan's completely inadequate wipers had never been one of its stronger points. 'What do you do when it rains?' A journalist had asked Neil. 'No worries, mate. I just drive a bit quicker – keeps the rain off fine…'

Joking was fine, but I was beginning to be a little concerned. 'Neil, are you OK?' I called over the radio. 'Yes, mate, having a good old chase with a Porsche…' Even in these awful conditions, there was just no stopping Neil. 'Take it easy, Neil,' I pleaded.

I was glued to the screens. Somebody came up behind me, tapping me on the shoulder to get my attention. As I looked round, I took off the headset so I could hear what he was saying. At that moment, I heard a chilling shout, coming from our friends in the Martin Short camp, right next door to us. 'Oh God! The Morgan's crashed! The Morgan's crashed!' The voice was Martin's.

I raced next door. 'What? 'Where? How bad?' 'Couldn't see where, the camera only showed it for a second, but it looked bad…I'm sorry, David.'

The team was now desperately trying to reach Neil on the radio, without success.

The TV showed the crash again, in terrible, shocking slow motion. We didn't see an impact, just the stomach-wrenching sight of the Morgan spinning several times and smashing into the barriers at the side of the track before coming to a stop. There was no sign of movement from the driver.

'Will somebody get hold of Neil, for Christ's sake!' I shouted. 'I need to know that he's OK.'

After an agonising few minutes, Neil finally called in. 'I'm OK,' he said. 'But the car's had it.'

The garage was suddenly packed with people, all wanting to know what had happened. I did a few press interviews, unable to tell them much more than the basic fact that we had crashed.

Then Neil came in. 'She bloody cut out on me!' He was quite shaken, though thankfully completely unhurt.

He had just overtaken a Porsche and tucked in front of it. The two cars had been racing hard up the hill in bad visibility, with the Porsche very close on Neil's tail. Then the Aero's engine had suffered a total power failure, causing the Porsche to collide with the back of the Morgan in a very high-speed impact. Neil had fought desperately to keep control, but was unable to stop the spin on the flooded track surface. The back of the car had hit the barriers hard at least three times, smashing the rear end of the car completely off. Even then, Neil had kept on trying to get started again, but it was all over.

Depression hit me like a train. Once again, we had tried our very best and once again the fates had dealt us a bitter blow. I felt desperately sorry, especially for poor Paula, who was all booted and suited ready for her first session of the race. Once again she was going home without racing the Morgan. Jacques, Eric and company were experienced racing hands and predictably, reacted very well. 'It's very bad luck, David, but you did your best. You will be back, I am sure,' said

A star in the car

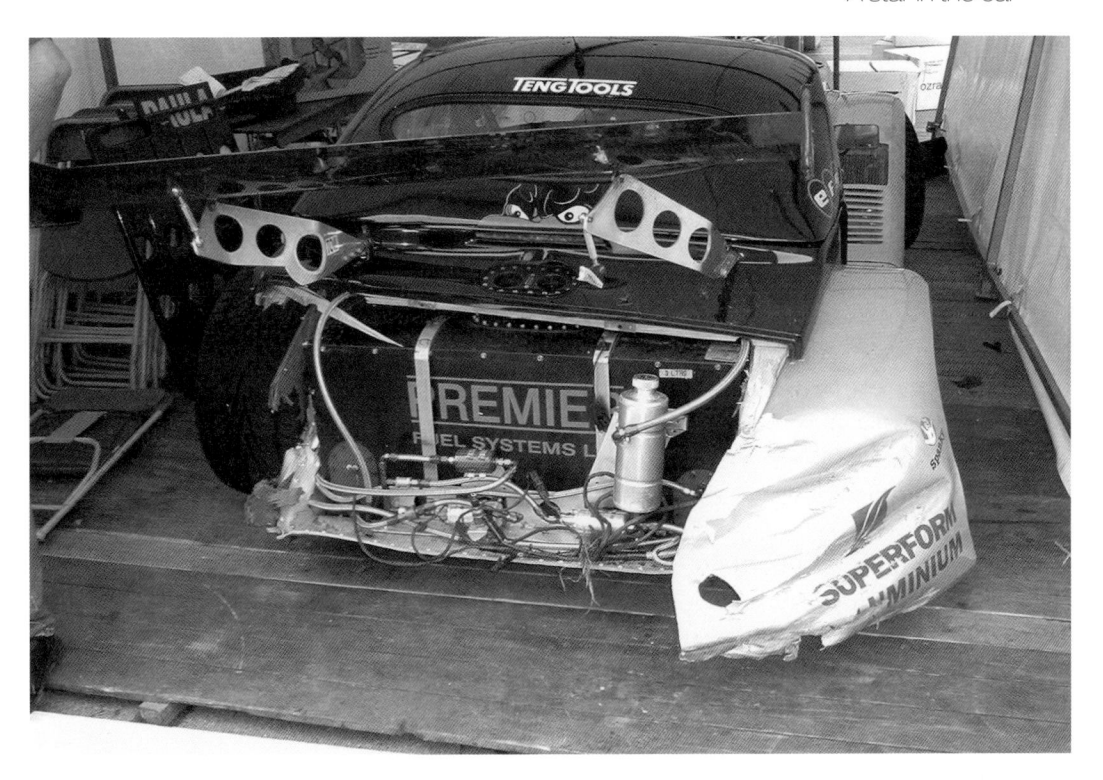

Above: Severe damage to the rear of the car after Neil's high-speed marriage to a Porsche. (DailySportsCar.com)

Right: The morning after the crash – with his mouth stuffed with straining credit cards, the team offers their manager the easy way out. (Anthony Harris)

87

Philippe. Hands were shaken all around and then suddenly the French delegation was gone. There was nothing left for us to do, except get the car safely back and locked away. In the morning, we would pack up and begin the long drive home.

I arrived home, exhausted and depressed. There had been plenty of time during the long drive through Europe to assess our situation and it looked very bleak indeed. Until the car was back in the workshop at Malvern, we would not know just how badly damaged it was; but from what we had already seen of it when the tangled mess of aluminium and wood was dragged back to the pit garage, it was pretty substantial damage.

In any case, the technical assessment was pretty academic. My hope, and our big gamble, had been that by putting on a good show at Spa (in presentational and performance terms) we would achieve good media coverage and therefore be in a stronger position to get sponsorship to go forward. I know Charles had high hopes about developing the relationship with Eric Sturzda; and Jonathon France and Paula had seemed likely to stay with us too. Now the whole plan was in tatters. We had been on the track for just a few hours and although Natasha and I had managed to get good mileage out of the Jacques Lafitte connection, our qualifying times had been only average. We could not expect to see glowing press reports. Worst of all, we seemed to be jinxed. No matter how hard we tried, it just kept going wrong. For myself, I was at a very low ebb and I simply did not know if I had the will or the energy to continue.

I unpacked the car, slept for 10 hours, then threw in another suitcase and drove up to Scotland to join my family, who were on holiday there. In hindsight, it is easy to see that I must have been quite a miserable holiday companion. The racing game was taking a big toll on those around me.

ten

Phoenix Rising

A week of pine scented air, no phone calls and wonderful scenery did a lot of good, but all too soon it was time to get back to work. While I had been away, others in the team had already made up their minds about where we were with the project after the crash. Crucially, Steve Lawrence had flown back to his home in California. Steve had been absolutely central to the building of the car and had done fantastic work. Without question, the greatly improved heat dispersion performance around the front of the car and through the drive train was directly down to him, as were many other more minor improvements from the 2002 design. He had spend literally hundreds of hours living with the car and grappling with enormous technical and commercial problems – not least the fact that we had never had enough money to do things properly. His position as Christopher's son was also important; it had added considerable weight to the project to have continuation of the Lawrence dynasty.

However, his departure had solved a tough management problem for me. While Steve had been quite superb during the development and build of the car, what I had seen at Spa had convinced me that he was not the person we needed to run the team during the race itself, had the project gone forward. I had not been looking forward to tackling such a thorny problem.

Rogier (the cabin boy) Vancamelbecke, Steve's essential right-hand man, had returned to his parents' home in Belgium directly after the race. Dave Bradley reverted to his consultancy work for Morgan Motor Company and others and Mark Baldwin went back to work managing Morgan's service operations. The rest of the team had been largely made up of 'mercenaries' and, as was their essential nature, they had moved on to the next billet.

So that was it. The team had dispersed; the workshop was empty and quiet. The money had run out. The poor, battered car rested on two trestle stands. It was a sad sight. Before packing up, the guys had removed some of the mangled bodywork and the true extent of the damage was now clear to see. The impact had sheered off the back of the car from just behind the rear wheel arches. The wooden superstructure had simply snapped cleanly off, while the boot compartment, along with the fuel tank and all the other expensive systems that it housed, were completely trashed.

I had a brief and sorry meeting with Charles Morgan, confirmed that I was resigning with immediate effect and handed over the chequebook and paperwork to him. I was genuinely sorry that I had not been able to produce a better result for him and for Morgan generally. But there was a silent agreement that enough was enough. Our luck had simply run out. It was the end of the road.

As I drove way from Malvern to pick up the pieces of my business and my personal life, my thoughts were interrupted by a phone call. It was Ben Coles, a freelance fabricator who had done quite a lot of work on the car. He had a thick Birmingham accent. 'Where are you?' he asked. 'Can you come back to the workshop?' Ben had gone in to collect his tools and was looking over the car.

I went back, thinking at least to say goodbye to him personally. I found him under the car, his feet sticking out from the side. 'All right, Dave?' he said. 'D' you want me to fix it then?'

'What do you mean 'fix it'?' I asked. 'It's had it, hasn't it?'

'Nah, mate. You'd be surprised what I can do with me welding kit. Won't be the first cut and shut I've done, not by a long way.'

This bombshell completely threw me. From a clear situation – we were absolutely finished, without hope – there was now a glimmer, however faint. I wasn't sure whether I was delighted or distraught to hear Ben's news. But I had heard it and there was no way to ignore it.

'You bastard!' I said, only half jokingly. 'You better work out what it might cost and let me know. But keep it to yourself for the moment, will you?'

I called Christopher and related what Ben had just told me. He too had assumed the game was up. 'I'd better come and have a look then,' he muttered. Christopher looked very carefully at the chassis and pronounced it basically sound. 'They're damned strong, these cars,' he said. 'If Ben says he can sort it out, I don't see why not.'

This was complete madness. We had no team, no money and no prospect of sponsors. I didn't need to wait for Ben's estimate to realise that it was not going to be much under £10,000 to fully repair the car. We were now in September. If we were going to try to stay on the long path to a 2004 Le Mans entry, it was essential that we race at the 1,000km event at the Le Mans Bugatti Circuit in November – a matter of weeks away. The entry fees would need to be paid almost immediately and we would need a whole lot more money to run the race itself.

Madness, indeed. There is little doubt in my mind that by every 'normal' and 'reasonable' standard, the project should have been allowed to die quietly at that stage. Had it done so, I myself would probably not have gone on to lose a successful business, a good deal of money and suffer serious damage to my marriage and several friendships. But switching off a life-support machine when a loved one has been pronounced dead by two doctors is a very different proposition from pulling the plug while the patient still breathes – no matter how little hope there may be for recovery. The Morgan way is *never* to give up, not while there is even the slightest glimmer of hope. Somewhere along the road, this credo had got into my blood; now I had little choice but to follow it.

During all my time with Morgan, I had only exchanged a few brief words with Peter Morgan, Charles' father and the company's long-serving and very well-loved chairman. Although by now in his eighties and officially semi-retired, 'PM', as everyone knew him, would still come into the factory several times a week. I don't think much of what was going on ever escaped his keen eyes.

One Monday morning, when I had just returned after a weekend in Scotland at the Knockhill circuit, where in the British GT Championship Neil had finally and famously beaten the Porsche on whose tail he had been all season, I met PM in the car park at Malvern. 'Good morning, Mr Morgan,' I said brightly. 'Have you heard the news from Knockhill this weekend, sir?' He had not. I told him of Neil's battle and his final victory. 'Really?' he said, his eyes shining bright. 'Jolly good!' And he walked off. It was the last time I spoke with him. PM passed away a few weeks later.

A fortnight later, I was off again, this time to Brands Hatch to watch Neil Cunningham drive again in Richard Thorne's Aero 8 Cup Car in the final round of the British GT. Richard had been having a strong season, despite having constantly to struggle to find finance for his project. His difficulties were similar to ours in the works team, although the amounts were smaller. Several different pay drivers had been in the car during the season, but Neil had been his stalwart ever since Donington. On this occasion, he had secured a young paying driver, Adam Sharpe, to share the drive with Neil and help cover the expenses. Adam's father, Robert Sharpe, was there to watch and we had a brief chat in the paddock.

He was clearly very ambitious for his son and indicated that if there was a chance of a Le Mans drive for Adam, he was prepared to help finance the project. We explored this a little further and the outline of a deal was struck. Robert would pay for Adam to drive in the 1,000km race and contribute towards Neil driving too. The payback for him would be the guarantee of a Le Mans seat for Adam with the Morgan Works Team – should we actually get there.

My mind raced as I drove home. There was now a real fighting chance – if we could fund the race entry fees and the repair of the car. I called Christopher to explain what I had just discussed with Robert Sharpe. 'Is he any good, this young bloke? We don't want any bloody whiz kids…' he asked immediately. 'He seems pretty sound, from what I've seen. And Neil rates him…'

'That's good enough for me,' Christopher replied. 'I will send in the entry fees tomorrow.'

This was an incredible act of faith and sheer guts; we still had no idea how we were going to pay for the repair work and race preparation, but Christopher knew, just as I did, that if we did not put our money (or more accurately, his money) on the table now, we would not get an entry for the 1,000km race – and effectively that meant no chance of a place at Le Mans.

We still needed a lot more financial support. Back in the office the following day, I racked my brains and contacts for some funding from somewhere. It was to prove a fateful day. There was no time to dither. Ben was in demand elsewhere and needed a decision right away if he was going to do the job. It was my turn to stick my neck out. I called Ben and told him to get moving. My own company, Transmission PR, was doing quite well and we would fund the work while we searched for a sponsor. The project was back on track.

I met with Charles to bring him up to date. He was happy to facilitate the new plan by allowing us free use of the car and the workshop, but was absolutely adamant that neither Morgan Motor Company or Aero Racing, the company he had originally set up to build race cars, would contribute any further funds to the project. I assured him that we would go ahead with Transmission and Robert Sharpe managing the project between us.

Christopher went off on holiday to America. The chemotherapy had left him very weak, but it seemed to have done its work and the cancer was in retreat. But while he was staying with friends in California, he suddenly became very ill indeed. Now it was his heart. Weakened by the cancer and the treatment, it was close to switching off permanently. Carey, his long-suffering wife, told me later that Christopher had been warned by his doctors not to travel, but of course he was having none if it. Now he was forbidden from flying and he could do nothing but sit there by the pool and get better. It was a strange twist of fate; it had to take an extraordinary set of circumstance to make Christopher rest properly. This time, he simply had no choice.

I was now constantly on the phone to Robert Sharpe. It was immediately clear that he was not the sort of sponsor to be at all happy with a 'hands off' relationship. In fact, as each day went past in a frenzy of negotiations and arrangements, it became apparent that he intended to keep a very tight grip on his money indeed. He insisted on negotiating with major suppliers himself and paying them direct. As he knew little or nothing about what we actually needed, I felt this was dangerous. Alarm bells rang a few times, but we somehow established a working protocol to deal with the major areas of expenditure. He would find transport and essential equipment to borrow or hire if necessary. As I already knew the Le Mans area, I would sort out hotels. In a portent of what was to come, catering was immediately a major area of disagreement. After the superb service we had received at Spa, I was adamant that we should use the same suppliers. Robert did not like their quote at all and wanted to self-cater somehow. We argued long and hard. Eventually I won.

The interior alarm bells grew louder. I no longer felt that I had full control of the team's destiny. But I was also aware that Robert's appearance on the scene had been critical; without it, the project would simply not have continued. I have no doubt that Robert had reached a similar conclusion. Whether we liked it or not, we needed each other. There was little enough time to worry about such matters. In the workshop, Ben was doing an amazing job; he was turning out to be an absolute genius in his field. Rogier was persuaded back from Belgium and was now working flat out on a deep race preparation programme. Dave Bradley had sent various parts of the engine wiring loom and the data system off to specialist laboratories for detailed analysis in an attempt to track down the mysterious cut-out that had plagued us. Worryingly, the tests were inconclusive. 'We can't find a bloody thing wrong,' Bradders told me. 'The only consistent thing about the failures seems to be that they only happen on weekend dates, never during the week!' In the end, the looms were completely replaced and extra shielding added. All we could do was to hope that we had sorted it.

Robert informed me that he had done a deal with one of the big 'professional' race teams; this included the hire of their race truck and some pit equipment, plus two men who would drive the truck and stay on to work with us. This team had run the winning Bentley Team at Le Mans the previous year. It was going to be interesting to see what they made of Morgan Works. Those annoying alarm bells reached a crescendo when Robert informed me that he had also secured the services of their Team Manager as a 'consultant' for the race weekend. Hiring in logistics and labourers was one thing; bringing in senior managers was quite another. I saw dark thunderclouds over the horizon.

The car was eventually ready and we went off to Pemburey in Wales for a shakedown test. Once again, the trusty old van and trailer were coaxed into action. Pemburey is a bleak, cold and wet place in early November. We had chosen it because it was very cheap for testing and Neil lived not far away. There are only two garages available at the circuit and when we arrived both were occupied. We had no covering at all and the whole team was quickly soaked to the skin from working in the pouring rain. However, the car was running fine. It was fantastic to see her come back to life. Neil reported no after effects from the crash and there was no sign of the engine issue. 'Yeah, but it's Thursday today, isn't it?' Bradders grinned.

Christopher, now back from America and slowly getting stronger, arrived with a very welcome hamper of hot coffee and rolls and we were all huddled in the back of the empty trailer sheltering from the pouring rain when a car pulled up next to our forlorn little camp. Two men got out and shuffled in with us. They introduced themselves to us as 'The Bentley Boys'. These were Robert's conscripts.

I should have loved to have been a fly on the wall inside their car as they drove home after spending an hour or so testing with the Morgan Works Team in the bucketing Welsh rain. They had looked at the car in silence; cast a barely disguised disparaging eye over our pathetic array of kit – the battered old toolboxes, rusty gas bottles and assorted blocks of wood and quickly made their farewells.

'I bet their catering budget was more than we have to spend on the whole project,' I said to the guys. This was later to become quite an effective line in our media activity.

eleven

Licence to kill

On the appointed day, a huge, gleaming, silver race truck pulled up at the Morgan factory. It swallowed up the car and all the kit with ease and the Bentley Boys set off for the drive down to Le Mans. The rest of the mechanics travelled in a hired minibus, while Bradders, Rogier and Mark Baldwin went in my car. We took a wrong turn somewhere, and we ended up going via Paris, which is definitely not the best route to Le Mans from Dover. Consequently, it was very late by the time we arrived in Le Mans. Luckily, we knew a bar that would still be open. We met up with our team mates and sank a couple of well-needed beers together in jolly mood. A little later, the Bentley Boys caught up with us. 'Don't worry, lads,' they announced. 'We've got a strategy all worked out…' This was so shocking, so totally out of order, that it was intensely funny and we all fell about laughing as soon as they had left. Our amusement continued early the following morning, as we waited outside in the minibus for the Bentley Boys to appear. When they finally came out of the hotel, each was carrying a large, officious looking aluminium briefcase.

'What do you reckon they've got in there, then?' said someone form the back of the team bus. 'Bloody sandwiches, probably!' came the quick-fire answer. The bus was still howling with laughter as the unknowing subjects of the derision boarded the bus.

I believe that in a race team – and this is probably so in any other close-knit team situation – ego is the enemy. This is something of a dichotomy; the individuals who were involved in the team were each extraordinary in their own way, consummate experts in their field. But when people like this are truly good, they demonstrate their very superiority by showing great humility. They are good; they know it and so does each of their team-mates. They absolutely do not have to prove anything. And so, in a strange and wonderful way, everyone is important, but nobody is.

This delicate but essential balance is maintained by a number of mechanisms, but the primary tool is merciless piss-taking. Any lapse of humility, however slight, is immediately and ruthlessly put down. On one occasion, one of the younger members of the team talked to me in private about how the put-downs were getting to him. I pointed out that if his mates were expending energy on putting him down, it meant that deep down they respected him – otherwise they simply would not bother. 'Take it and learn to give some back,' was the best advice I could give him.

There is another thing in which I strongly believe. In management speak, it is known as 'empowerment'. In practice, it means leaving people alone unless they clearly want and need some input. To take the Bentley Boys as an example, here was a real potential for trouble. They were outsiders, who did not know the way the team functioned and worse, much worse, they thought they knew it all. I could have intervened formally at an early stage, but I had complete faith that the Morgan Team would sort it out very effectively, in their own time and in their own way. The result would be a stronger one and I like to think that by not interfering I gained a little more respect from the team. Many managers do not seem to be able to leave people alone enough.

Most race teams I had come across were run by one strong character, usually with some kind of technical background. The larger teams would have a team manager, who would largely be responsible for commercial, administrative, logistics and PR functions and there would also be a race engineer, who was responsible for the technical aspects of running the car. I never made any secret of the fact that I had little or no technical knowledge and we certainly were not in a position to employ a race engineer. So, like every other aspect of our activity, things were done differently in the Morgan Team.

Technical decisions on the car were arrived at via a process, rather than the dictatorial belief of any one individual. I had worked hard (and argued with Robert even harder about the need and the cost of doing so) to bring in specialist expertise in the form of Mick Boasman, a data analysis wizard from Magnetti Marelli, and Lutz Passon, a suspension specialist working with the German suspension experts, KW. These two experts, working closely with Bradders, Mark Baldwin and Rogier and using Neil as a superb test and development driver, formed the core technical 'committee' that took major decisions about set-up and performance, with the huge experience and design knowledge about the Aero 8 that Christopher could provide in the background. I saw my own role in this process as one of overall facilitator and arbitrator; in many ways an extension of the empowerment philosophy. This approach also enabled me to concentrate more on the equally important functions of PR and team logistics.

Others, though, had little or no faith in our game plan. Robert was increasingly demonstrating that he believed we needed someone from the outside who 'knew what they were doing technically'; hence his insistence on bringing in the team manager from the ex-Bentley Team. This was based on a misunderstanding of how the Morgan Works Team functioned. It was also fundamentally flawed. Robert's own lack of experience of the running of a race team was very apparent; the man he had drafted in was not a 'Race Engineer', he was a 'Team Manager'. It was not at all clear how this was going to be resolved.

Rogier 'the cabin boy' Vancamelbecke (left) and ace fabricator Ben Coles hard at work preparing the car for scrutineering for the 1000k race. (David Dowse)

We were back at the Le Mans Circuit and I put the politics aside for the time being. Entering the paddock once again immediately invoked the unique magic of the place. Even with the stands completely empty and the track silent, the pit straight seemed to bathe in history and drama. The guys were unusually quiet, too, and I knew that I was not alone in my feelings. But there was not much time to dwell on such ethereal matters. There was work to do; a full day's hard graft setting up the pit garage and preparing for the inevitable joys of scrutineering the following day.

We were now firmly back under the auspices of the ACO; this event was to be run under full Le Mans 24 Hours regulations. This meant that even though we had enjoyed a relatively painless journey through scrutineering just a few weeks previously at Spa, we had no idea how we would fare here. The rulebook came out for the hundredth time and we went over the car yet again, from stem to stern. I was far more nervous at this time than I would have cared to admit to anyone; if we had a major problem at scrutineering this time, suicide would not have seemed an unreasonable option.

The pit set up went well and just as I had hoped, the Bentley Boys were soon sorted out as Bradders, Mark Baldwin and Rogier Vancamelbecke asserted themselves in their inimitable way. The catering rig arrived on time and was set up a short distance away. We closed the garage door as the sun set and headed off to talk endlessly and happily about the car over beers and food in town. We heard no more from the Bentley Boys about race strategy.

The ACO likes to do things in a stylish way. Not for them scrutineering in a shed somewhere on the circuit. Instead we were required to ship the car to a large, modern factory unit a couple of miles from the circuit. Inside the vast space, the various scrutineering stations were set up, with their specialist ramps and measuring equipment. A large crowd had come to witness the whole circus and an array of media and photographers hovered about. I stayed with the car and the technical team, while Robert went into the administrative sign-on room with the two drivers. We were making good progress through the technical tests. The scrutineers seemed warm and friendly; a marked contrast from what we had experienced at Donington. The phone rang. It was Robert. He sounded very agitated. 'You had better get in here fast,' he said menacingly.

Neil and Adam were at the driver sign in desk and there was indeed a problem. Quite a major one. Their race licences, which were perfectly valid for racing in the British GT and at the Spa circuit, were not valid for the Le Mans circuit, which demanded an 'international C' status. Both our drivers had only 'international B' status. I could not believe we had made such a stupid error. It had never crossed my mind that the drivers would not know what they needed to enter the race and ensure that they had the correct credentials. Adam, and to a lesser degree Neil too, were very much Robert's property. But it had happened on my watch and as team manager ultimately I would take the blame. Certainly Robert left me in no doubt at the time that this was his own conclusion.

But this was not the time for recriminations. We needed solutions and we needed them fast. Robert, Neil and myself spent the next several hours on the phone to the UK, trying to track down the officials who could upgrade the licences. It was a terribly frustrating process. There was no question at all that both drivers had more than enough experience to qualify for the 'international C' status, but they had to prove it. Then the correct official had to sign off the upgrade and fax it to us.

There was nothing to do but wait a few hours while it got sorted out. Robert was furious and clearly believed this was ample proof that we could not be trusted to do anything right. He went back to the circuit and huddled together with his 'consultant' team manager. A couple of hours later, he triumphantly appeared, clutching the vital fax confirmation and claiming that his man had sorted it all out. I honestly believe that it was under control anyway, but I was only interested in the facts; that little problem was now solved.

However, after scrutineering, we were faced with another, equally threatening issue that was going to be a little more difficult to solve. The car had sailed through all the major scrutineering stations, until one of the officials casually put a ruler across the rear wheel. He stroked his moustache, measured again and then called two colleagues over to join him. Something was clearly amiss.

Nerves stretched to the limit as the Aero 8 enters scrutineering for the 1000k race. (Melissa Warren)

A little nod to history – the DeWalt race truck in the background as the Morgan Works car awaits its turn for scrutineering. (Melissa Warren)

Neil Cunningham talks to the media following scrutineering with Adam Sharpe. (Melissa Warren)

The final report cleared the car completely, apart from one small but rather critical issue; the rear wheels were an inch larger than the regulations allowed. How the hell could that have happened? Having been accused by Robert, at least by implication, of incompetence over the matter of the licences, here we were, about to confirm his darkest suspicions. It was my turn to get furious.

The wheels for the car are very specialised and of course extremely expensive. They have to be ordered – and paid for – many months in advance, in our case from a supplier in Italy. The wheels in question had in fact been ordered long before I had joined the project and somehow, during the repeated technical checks and measurements we had made at the factory, the size of the rear wheels had been missed. I suspect that everybody assumed that something so fundamental had to be correct – especially as Christopher himself had ordered the wheels. Whatever the reason, we were once again in deep trouble.

We did not have enough spare wheels of the correct size to run the race. Race wheels have specialist fittings that are specifically made for the car; so despite the fact that many of the other teams in the paddock were running wheels made by the same supplier, there was no chance that we could beg or borrow some extra wheels. We gathered together for a crisis meeting. All other options being quickly eliminated, we were left with only one chance: somehow we would have to get some wheels from the factory out to Le Mans – and quickly. What followed was an incredible demonstration of the deep well of resource that the Morgan Team could call upon. We may have had almost no money, but what we did have was goodwill and commitment in abundance and these true riches were what mattered now.

It being late on Friday afternoon, the Morgan factory was already closed. Steve Morris, the long-suffering factory manager, was tracked down on his mobile, our perilous situation quickly explained and the solution outlined. He immediately agreed to go back into the factory, open up, find the wheels we needed and load them onto the small flatbed truck that served as a factory workhorse.

Step one was under control. He had already given up his Friday evening without a murmur and I have no doubt that Steve would have driven the truck down himself, but he had important family commitments that weekend. We needed someone to leave within a couple of hours, drive through the night down to Dover, catch an hour's sleep on the boat, then continue driving all night down to Le Mans – all in, around ten hours of uncomfortable, slow driving. At such short notice, this was going to be a pretty tough job to fill.

Once again, my brother-in-law Tim came to our rescue. I quickly explained the situation to him and the vital importance of the truck getting to Le Mans at the absolute earliest opportunity in the morning. Being the solid brick that he is, Tim made no fuss at all and was on the road to Malvern to collect the truck within minutes of the call. I made some more calls to get the ferry times for Tim, sent them to him by text message and that was it. An hour of frantic phone calls – and the willingness of some special individuals to go the extra mile – had once again kept us alive to fight another day. Or so I fervently hoped. There were so many things that could go wrong during the night; missed ferries, customs problems, breakdowns, getting lost... any of these things and probably others I would rather not imagine might prevent Tim from making it in time. But there was nothing more I could do. Tim's mobile would not work after he left the UK, so I was in the dark until he arrived at the circuit. I slept as best I could.

Saturday dawned – a cold but dry November morning. We were at the pits very early, ready for a big day ahead of us. I was drinking a third cup of coffee when a familiar form appeared. 'Tim!' I said, very warmly. 'You're making a bit of a habit of this!' At this point, I should like to register our thanks to the people at Dunlop Tyres, who overnight had somehow managed to find us rubber to fit the new rim size.

We had the correct licences. We had the correct wheels. All our paperwork checked out. Finally, we could get on with the important business of making the car go faster.

Finally ready to roll – pre-race dramas over. (David Dowse)

twelve

Back on track

During the day, two full 3-hour practice sessions were scheduled. Our game plan was to use this time to the utmost advantage to do some proper development work. Mick Boasman arrived and Lutz, our German suspension expert, turned up with his support van. For the first time, we could make full use of our expensive data acquisition system. The first session started and we were on track on time. After Neil's shakedown laps, he emerged grinning from ear to ear. 'She's going bloody good, mate!' he mumbled from inside his helmet.

The game plan was simple; we would go out for three or four laps, come in, download the data, analyse it, make any indicated changes to suspension and other settings and go out for another three or four laps. This process would continue, barring any other issues, all through the 3-hour session. Both Neil and Adam would also get plenty of seat time.

It went like a dream. Each time we made changes recommended by Lutz or Mick, we knocked a couple of seconds off the best lap time and soon we were circulating well within the class spectrum. The engine was running perfectly. Bradders announced himself very happy with the temperature data and there was absolutely no sign of the electronics gremlin. The end of the practice sessions found a very happy team in the Morgan camp. It had been by far the best day we had ever experienced on a racetrack. We had logged a perfectly respectable time and the car was running very reliably. We had earned a beer or two that night.

But first, there was some tyre change practice to be done.

Christopher had drummed into my head the basic truth of endurance racing: 'It's not won on the track; it's lost in the pits.' Coming from such an experienced hand, I had no difficulty in taking this mantra to heart.

Maths has never been my strongest point, ever since those '…could do better,' reports at school. Actually, I did do rather better in English, so thank you, Mr Poulton.

But even I could do the basic arithmetic required here. Assuming the car circulates at around the average of the class times, the first big consideration is reliability. If the car keeps going, without major repairs being required, you are

Above: Adam Sharpe mixing it with one of the Porsches during practice at the 1000k. (Melissa Warren)

Below: Refuelling practice at the 1000k. It's a long stretch to reach over the rear wing and dock the fuel line.

over the biggest hurdle. To put this in context; even a relatively minor repair – say, replacing a broken windscreen – can cost the team 10 minutes or so extra time in the pits. With only a matter of seconds separating the lap times of cars on the track, it doesn't take an Einstein to work out that you have to go very fast indeed to have any chance of catching up even 10 minutes of lost time. So reliability is absolutely fundamental. It's one of the things that make endurance motor racing so different from anything else. Once you have reliability under your belt, the next relevant factor is fuel and tyre consumption; the territory of the scheduled pit stop. What you are looking for is as few of these as possible. If you can run for longer on one tank of fuel and one set of tyres, you can gain time in the pits that would simply be impossible to gain on the racetrack.

These factors make the endurance race a fascinating combination of strategy and coping with the unknown. In our class, the LMGT, Porsche has made the practice of running endurance races into something beyond an art form. The cars generally run like clockwork machines that very rarely breakdown. They are relatively light on fuel and tyres and you could set your watch against their planned pit stop strategies. With many years of well-resourced, factory-backed development behind them, they are also very quick. This means that unless they are very unfortunate and suffer a rare breakdown or a major incident on the circuit, a Porsche will probably win. Period.

Relatively speaking, we were at the very beginning of the development of a totally new and radical car. We had not yet even passed the engine reliability issue and years of development, along with many hundreds of thousands of pounds to fund it, would be required before the car could hope to reach its pinnacle of performance.

In all this discussion I have not mentioned the drivers. While the strategy I've just outlined assumes that a driver is competent, he or she actually has very little opportunity to have a real impact on the outcome of the race – unless it is in a negative way. What you require of the driver is above all to keep out of trouble; to avoid contact with other cars and keep the car on the tarmac.

In endurance racing, bravado and the desperate 'will to win' – normally so vital in sports – can actually be the enemy. It takes quite a special driver to understand this, to accept a brief from the team to run more slowly than the driver knows he is capable of driving; to preserve the engine, keep fuel consumption down, etc. Many drivers, especially the less experienced ones, are simply not capable of doing this. It goes against their basic, winning instincts.

In our case, Adam Sharpe demonstrated maturity well beyond his nineteen years of age; although it's probably true to say that his vehemently ambitious, sponsoring father had more difficulty with the concept of endurance racing.

For Robert, the concept that we were quite openly entering a race with little or no hope of winning it was probably approaching blasphemy. For him, winning was everything. Second was simply nothing. As I frequently said in media interviews at the time, for the Morgan Team, with our comparatively tiny funding, starting the race was a victory in itself; finishing it – in any position – would be cause for great celebration.

There is a fault line here that needs exploring in greater depth. The whole concept of the Morgan Works Team was founded on an impossible dream – that if you tried long and hard enough you could overcome tremendous adversity. This was the Morgan Way, with a unique heritage stretching back to the pioneering days of motoring. What inspired and drove me – and I think most of the key players in the team – was simply the chance to carry this banner, represented by the famous Morgan winged logo, back to the spiritual home of endurance racing. In our case, the clichéd concept of 'just taking part' really did matter.

It is not for me to criticise anyone who did not feel the same way about our mission. Certainly there were other agendas in play. But I admit I often seriously wondered whether we would find sufficient common ground. It is a matter of motivation and kismet. We had found from the beginning that if we kept our motivation clear, help came to us. I knew instinctively that the moment we introduced ego, the motivation would be corrupted and the help would cease.

But let's get back to our tyre changes. From the discussion above, it is hopefully clear that time spent in the pits is critical. And it is the unscheduled stops – to fix things that go wrong during the race – that are the really critical ones. However, the scheduled stops, to change tyres, drivers and to refuel, are also important; the shorter they are the better.

Now, at this point, something else enters the equation: the pit crew's pride in their work. During the race, the crew running the front of the pits is very much on show. It really is a stage; complete with bright lights, TV and stills cameras and a huge audience in the stands opposite. This is the crew's payback time. All their hard, dirty graft and impossibly long working hours are behind them once a race starts. Now it's show time. And they really want to shine. This means that there is a much more pressing imperative than simply saving a few seconds in the tyre change. They want to do it the best; and in our case, the Morgan boys had an additional dimension to their performance. They might be the vagabonds of the paddock, but they were determined to show the 'big boys' that Morgan could mix it with the best in the world. There was yet another degree of pride – and rivalry – in play. For the tyre change, the car is effectively split into two teams, one working the driver's side and the other the offside. Whichever side you're on, you want more than anything to do it quicker than your mates on the other side.

And so to the practice. The car was precisely placed in the working area of the pit lane, just where it would be in the race. Airlines and spare wheels were laid out and the team huddled around discussing how they were going to approach the job. The whole operation has to be conducted under strict rules that determine how many people and which individuals can be involved at each point and where equipment has to be stored.

I watched from a distance. Unlike all of the other teams in the paddock, Morgan Works was not a team that had worked together for a long time and so it had not yet melded into a cohesive unit. The Bentley Boys, with their 'status' and experience, were making their views known to the Morgan personnel. The atmosphere was a becoming a little fractious. Once again, I decided to stay in the background and simply observe.

The game plan was agreed, with the Bentley Boys having won round one. '3, 2, 1…GO!' I shouted, hitting the stopwatch start button.

The first try was a shambles. But they did it again and again and eventually hit a reasonable time for the whole process. It wasn't bad. It wasn't particularly good, either. They huddled around again. The temperature of the argument was rising a little. Mark Baldwin, usually so unflappable, was not a very happy man. People were getting tired, hungry and above all thirsty for the beers they knew were waiting for them. It was time to intervene.

'Good work, guys,' I said. 'We'll wrap it up soon, but before we go, let's just try it Mark's way a couple of times.'

Mark took charge, in his inimitably gentle but steely way. They duly rearranged the plan and the layout. '…GO!' I shouted. On the very first run through, the time was cut to under half what it had been working the 'Bentley' way.

'Beer o'clock, I think, gentlemen,' said Bradders. No one argued with him.

It had been a really good day and it could not have ended better. There can be few things more satisfying than a cold beer at the end of a very long day at a race circuit.

And tomorrow was race day.

A journalist once asked Christopher Lawrence what it had been like in the 1962 Le Mans race when he had won the 2-litre class. 'Pretty bloody boring, actually,' was his characteristically blunt reply. 'Nothing much happened. We drove all day and all night, came in for tyres and fuel and that was that. Won the race, packed up and drove the car back to England the next day!' This was the stuff of legend, of course, but there is a very valid point here. In endurance racing, what you actually want is nothing to report. It means nothing has gone wrong.

During the 2003 1,000km Le Mans Endurance Series race, nothing went wrong. The car performed faultlessly and the team were unimpeachable. Sitting in the motor home, I wrote the first positive race report press release of the Morgan Works Team's short history:

The Morgan Works Race Team finished the inaugural event of the European Le Mans Series at Le Mans Bugatti Circuit in a highly creditable 8th in class position among a strong field of 18 entries in the GT Class.

The result sends a loud and clear signal that the Works Team, which has endured major technical and funding hurdles during 2003, is now a serious contender at the highest level of international endurance GT racing – a formula that is growing fast and becoming a flagship series in the motorsport arena.

Team Manager David Dowse comments:

'It was a very tough race, on a challenging circuit and with a field that included the best GT cars in the world. The Aero 8 ran absolutely faultlessly for six hours in gruelling conditions. Our drivers Neil Cunningham and Adam Sharpe did a really professional job and the pit crew, which is just as important as the car and drivers in endurance racing, were awesome. We came here to prove that we are a credible force and I think we have done that in no uncertain terms.'
Ends

There was one blot on our new, rosy skyline, and not for the first or the last time it concerned catering. After the superb service we had received at Spa, I had fought a long and hard fight with Robert to use the same supplier for the Bugatti race weekend. Robert had strongly objected to the costs, even after he had managed to knock down the original price. This being November, I knew

On track to a turning point in the whole campaign; the Aero 8 storms on through the night at the Bugatti 1000k. (Melissa Warren)

that hot food was going to be very important and I also knew how difficult it would be to keep running outside to bring in takeaways, which was one of Robert's preferred alternatives. I had stood my ground. The team had supported me. Robert had very reluctantly capitulated.

All should have been fine. It was not. The woman who ran the catering business was double booked that weekend and instead of coming herself sent a friend in her place. The result was a poor shadow of what we had been given at Spa, leaving the team disappointed and me with a substantial egg on my face with Robert. It was an issue that was soon to come back to bite me again.

Before we left the circuit, Robert and I sat down for a critical private business meeting. The gist of the discussion was simple; I had now been working almost full time on team affairs for about ten months with no payment and had also spend many thousands of my own money that I needed to get back somehow. Robert had come along at a critical moment and injected money to make the Bugatti race possible. I told him that there was no chance at all that Morgan Motor Company would fund any part of an on-going campaign. If we were going to go forward, we would need to formalise things somehow.

Robert seemed very prepared for this conversation and its content. It did not take us long to shake hands on the outline of an arrangement. We would agree that what each of us had contributed – time from me and cash from Robert – would be treated as equivalent investments to create a new, 50/50 business entity. This seemed fair enough to me, but I had one further request. 'I'd like to give Bradders and Mark Baldwin a small shareholding, so they are totally involved.' I said.

'No, they get paid for what they do. The business club is closed.' His voice had certain finality about it. Robert was a man who was used to getting his own way. I decided to leave it at that for the moment. There would be time later to revisit the idea, when we formalised the papers. We had turned a corner. But where would the road lead us next?

The true importance of what happened at the Bugatti race cannot be overestimated. Quite simply, if we had not done well, our chances of a successful application for a 2004 Le Mans 24 Hours entry would have been zero. But there was still a terribly long way to go. To 'tick all the boxes' and build the unassailable case that I was determined to make, we would need to climb another mountain in the foothills of Le Mans – the 12 Hours of Sebring, in Florida.

thirteen

Diversion down under

But first, there was to be a slight diversion. Actually, quite a long diversion; to the other side of the world, in fact. To Australia and the 24 Hour race at Bathurst. What happened next was due in part to a strategy that I had cooked up with Charles Morgan and Christopher at the outset. We had agreed that there was a lot of potential benefit to be gained from gently blurring the distinction between the Morgan Works Team proper – the team that raced the Le Mans car – and the private teams running the Cup cars in both the UK and the USA. It had been an inspired move by Charles to produce several race cars in the same blue and silver two-tone livery carried by the Works car itself. I had immediately picked up on this as a very helpful PR tool; pictures of a blue and silver Morgan in action would inevitably be perceived by the public as one and the same race car. There should be benefits for everyone; the private teams would gain additional kudos, the Works Team would appear to be rather more active than it actually was and above all, the Morgan brand was the umbrella for it all. It was a smart plan.

However, there were inevitable problems. With Neil and Adam now driving regularly for both the Works Team and Richard Thorne's British GT team, there was a real potential for confusion in the media and the minds of the public. As I was now quite well known in my role as team manager for the Works team and I had very often been present at British GT events throughout the season, the lines became more blurred than we had intended.

Robert's family had strong personal links in Australia. Neil had grown up there. Very soon after the Bugatti race, Robert started talking excitedly about the prospect of taking part in the Bathurst race. The Works Team would have loved to have taken it on; our tails were up and most of us had never been to Australia. But this was simply a bridge too far. There were many reasons why; the primary one being the engine. The Mader race engines we used in the Works car cost £75,000 a piece. We only had two of them and with quite a few test and race hours already notched up, we simply could not afford to expend an engine in a 24-hour race – especially a race that would do nothing to move us closer to our Le Mans goal. It was a no brainer, as they say in Florida.

But there was no stopping Robert. He had set his heart on going to Bathurst. Several things then happened in quick succession. First, I heard from a media contact that Robert had done a deal to race at Bathurst in a different car – I believe it may have been a Porsche – with Adam and Neil driving. I was a little surprised to hear this news, but it was of little consequence; it did not impact on any of our plans for Morgan Works. The next news, just a couple of days later, was important and it certainly did have the potential to impact on our planning. Robert had pulled out of the original deal and instead agreed with Richard Thorne to go to Bathurst with the Morgan GT Cup car. What was more, the entry was listed as 'Morgan Works'.

My mind raced to take on board the implications of this development. The first and biggest concern was the car. The Cup car, though visually quite similar to the Works car, was actually a completely different animal. It was designed to race in short, sprint races – something that it had proved very good at during the British GT season that had just ended. But surely this was a crazy decision. Did Robert – and Richard Thorne, who surely should know better – think that we had spend two years and hundreds of thousands developing an endurance race car just for the fun of it? Why would we do so if the job could be done by a Cup car costing a fraction of that?

The Works car was built from the ground up to do a 24-hour racing job. Every component in it had been selected for durability. Hundreds of hours of work, including wind tunnel analysis, had gone into ensuring that the drive train would stay cool. It had a gearbox that would not disgrace a small tank and armoured fuel and oil lines and wiring looms throughout; all specially routed to avoid heat and wear.

To take a Cup Class car, which was effectively a stripped-down road car with an upgraded engine and suspension, to a 24-hour race on one of the world's most demanding circuits simply seemed like madness; and worse, it made a mockery of everything we had done on the Works project. I began seriously to question whether my new partner in the Morgan Works project had any idea what he was doing.

But the entry was already in. It was Robert's money and Richard's car. There was nothing I could do about it. However, I was determined that I would keep hold of the PR reins and this meant a trip to Australia.

On the long flight, I reflected on the frantic events of the past few months. This was to be a refreshing experience for me; I was looking forward to seeing a little of Australia and for the first time since the 2002 Le Mans race that had started it all, I was travelling to an event where I was not responsible for anything other than the press and media activity.

We arrived at Sydney very early on a Sunday morning. Dazed and confused from jetlag, there was great confusion as the various hire cars and a minibus were acquired. I have never liked not being in full control of my destiny and here I was on the other side of the world, with no knowledge about the onward schedule and certainly no control over it.

Eventually we were all aboard one or another form of transport, to be whisked off through the still sleeping streets of Sydney to the waterfront. A couple of hours of wandering aimlessly around mostly closed shops followed before we were herded aboard a ferry for the trip across the harbour to Manley Beach. The iconic site of the Opera House and the Harbour Bridge glistening in the early sunshine was quite memorable and my spirits lifted, as they always do when I'm on or near the sea.

The almost comical scene that followed when we disembarked onto the teeming pier at Manley surprised and shocked me. Robert, surrounded by the small crowd that was his entourage, loudly announced that we were to reassemble at this point at a given time – about 3 hours hence – and promptly disappeared off into the crowd at a rate of knots, with Kerstin trying to keep up with him. The rest of us – drivers, mechanics and assorted wives and girlfriends, were left, quite literally, to fend for ourselves. Most people had not even had the chance to change some money.

That evening, we were driven out of the city, to a small town some thirty miles inland. We checked into a cheap motel, where we were to spend 36 hours acclimatising and getting over the jetlag before moving up country to the Bathurst circuit – a further 3-hour drive into the mountains.

It was very hot and humid. The next morning, I wandered around the town, amazed by the incongruity of the Christmas displays in the gardens of the single-storey houses, surrounded by tropical foliage.

Back at the motel, I set up my notebook PC and started to work on some emails and press releases. There was no air-con in the stifling room, so I worked with the room door wide open. As I typed, a small movement caught the corner of my eye. I looked up and practically jumped out of the chair to the very back of the room. Coming around the back of the upright computer screen were two eyes on the end of large, flexing stalks. As I watched, incredulous, they were slowly followed by the head and body of an enormous stick insect, which casually settled on the computer keyboard. Welcome to Australia.

Later, I related this encounter to Neil. 'Jeez, mate, she was only a baby! You should see her mama…'

The following day, well rested, I was glad to be finally on the way to the circuit. We travelled in several vehicles. Robert, with Adam and other members of his family, had already gone ahead. I shared a car with Neil (who was the only one who knew the way) and a couple of mechanics. We were followed by another car carrying Tom Shrimpton – one of the two pay drivers Robert had signed up to drive in the race – and his parents.

When we were about an hour away from the circuit, Robert called me. He was very excited. 'There's TV everywhere, looking for us!' he sounded almost beside himself. 'Yes, Robert,' I replied, with exaggerated calm. 'That's because I've told them we're coming. Morgan is going to be big news here. I told you it would.'

'Now listen very carefully and under no circumstances are you to let anyone else in the car know what I'm saying. Understand?' he replied, his voice took on an almost vicious tone. 'I don't want anyone getting this coverage but Adam, understand?' I was completely taken aback. 'What?' 'You just do exactly what I tell you,' he commanded. There was that menace again, the same tone I had heard at the Bugatti scrutineering.

My instructions were to ensure that on arrival at Bathurst the Shrimptons went directly to their hotel, checked in and stayed there for at least an hour. I was then to go straight to the circuit and help with maximising Adam Sharpe's TV exposure.

I loathed being pulled into such a subterfuge, but was in no position to argue with Robert. So we found their hotel, a dingy-looking roadside motel and I suggested that they might like to chill out there for a while until we got things organised at the circuit.

When I arrived, a TV news crew was getting ready to shoot an interview with Adam, who was sitting in the car. This was home turf and I got on with my job straight away, noting with mild amusement Robert hanging around nearby in agitated excitement. He came over and whispered conspiratorially in my ear. 'Make sure they get his name in, won't you.' 'Yes, Robert.' I replied, thinking it was probably better not to tell him that it was the car they were really interested in.

As the cameras rolled, the Shrimpton's car pulled up and all three occupants got out. As they stood there watching, I felt a wave of guilt and shame and I silently vowed that I would never again allow myself to be railroaded in such a way.

As I had hoped and expected, the arrival of the Morgan in Australia attracted huge media attention. I had done some work before we left the UK to warm up the interest, but it was hardly an uphill battle. There is a small but fiercely loyal Morgan fan club in Australia and I had been in touch with them via the Owners Clubs. I am sure they did quite a lot of work stirring up interest, too. We certainly caught the Aussie imagination. During that first day at the circuit, I was busy with back-to-back TV and radio interviews and I was very happy getting on with my job and staying well out of the way of the management of the team and the set up.

To make the whole project possible, Robert had employed the services of Darrell Dixon, an Australian motorsport jack of all trades. Short, rotund and completely unstoppable, Darrell could and would do anything; from picking people up from the airport and booking hotels to arranging the freight logistics and sorting out problems with local customs officials or replacing a gearbox. He was as intensely intelligent and capable as he was completely without frills or pretensions. I have no idea of the details of the deal Robert had secured with him. However, from observation, it appeared that a single price had been agreed that would have to cover everything – car hire, catering, hotels, fuel, personnel,

Driver line up for the 2003 Bathurst 24 Hour race. From left to right: Tom Shrimpton, Adam Sharpe, Neil Cunningham and Keith Ahlers. (David Dowse)

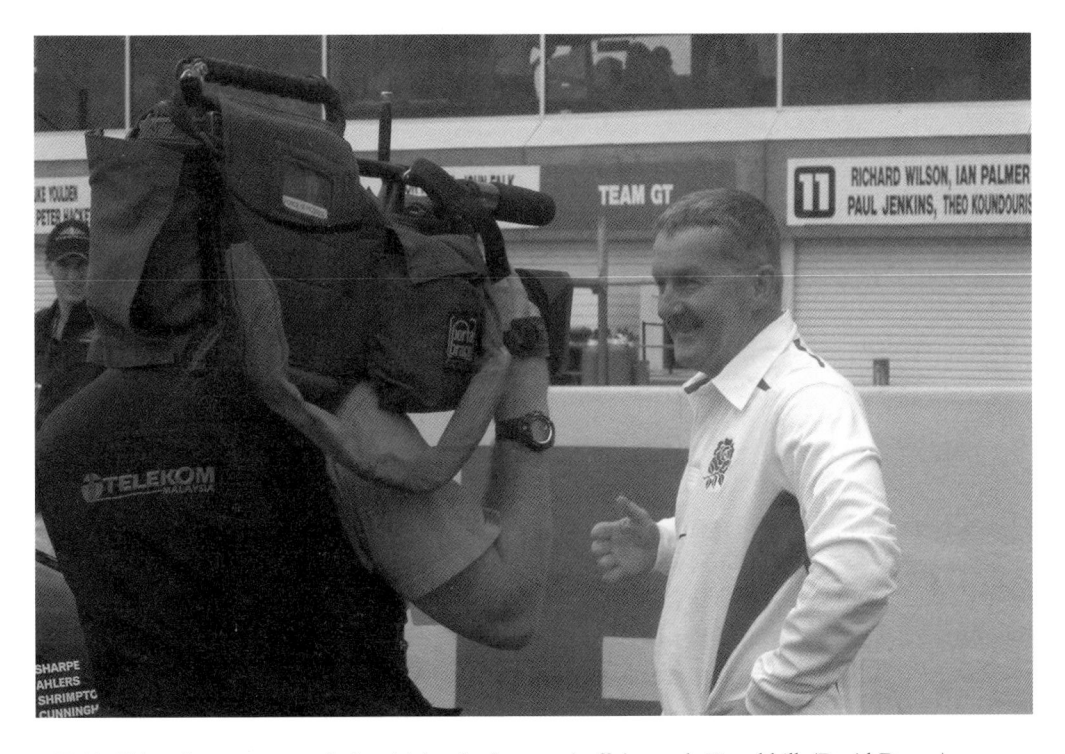

Keith Ahlers does a very professional job – both on and off the track. Knockhill. (David Dowse)

etc. One thing that I am certain about is that there would have been very little fat in the deal; Darrell would have to wheel, deal and work his butt off for every dollar and cent of his margin.

I was fascinated by this from an objective point of view and intrigued as to how it could possibly work. I knew enough about the economic realities of racing by this time to realise how tight it must be. The answer, at least in part, came when I found that virtually every one of the local mechanics and support staff were volunteers; working either for the love of being involved, or for love of Darrell – a large part of his extended family seemed to be involved at some stage.

Experience has shown me that whatever the situation, volunteers are usually a false economy. No matter how willing, they are simply not getting paid and there is a difference. That said, beggars cannot be choosers.

It was fascinating to see the differences between the European racing environment and the Australian way. There's an atmosphere about Australia which is quite enchanting; casual, relaxed informality balanced with the tough, outback survivor spirit. All of this was plain to see from the moment we arrived. People at every level – from the senior race authorities to the press office staff and even, most shockingly, the scrutineers, were genuinely friendly and welcoming. They were just delighted to have us along. It was a very refreshing antidote to our recent experiences back home.

The following day, the rest of the team arrived. Robert handed out some team clothing and I was horrified to see a completely new Morgan Works identity, combined with the bright orange of Adam Sharpe's own personal logo, all printed on black shirts. I had no idea that this was going to happen and I was very unhappy about it. It was time to confront Robert.

'Oh, no worries, mate; they're only for this race… we had to run something up in no time, so we just didn't have time to talk to you about it…' I didn't buy that and I didn't like the way things were developing. I resolved to try to keep things on the right track by keeping as tight a grip as possible on the PR output.

The Bathurst 24 Hours is run under local regulations, which allow for up to four drivers. This must have been critical to Robert's commercial plan, as it allowed him to sell two additional seats alongside Adam and Neil. I've already mentioned Tom Shrimpton, a quiet, intelligent seventeen-year-old who had been doing very well in his first season in the British GT. Keith Ahlers was to complete the line up and a more contrasting team-mate could hardly be imagined.

A veteran of hundreds of races at every level, Keith was one of the best known and respected names in the Morgan world. A true enthusiast, he owned several Morgan road and race cars and had been competing all season against Richard Thorne in the British GT Championship, driving his own Aero 8 Cup car. It was good to have a proper 'Morganeer' aboard. I had met Keith before, but in Australia I was able to get to know him and his wife Sue a little better. It was an enjoyable experience.

Billy Bellinger keeps a watchful eye over Keith Ahlers in the Bathurst pit lane. (Melissa Warren)

Scrutineering, practice and qualifying went without incident. All four drivers came out the car after each session practically glowing with pleasure. I was about to find out why. My friends in the media office, where I had spent a lot of time during the first days at the circuit, kindly offered me a rare opportunity to go around the circuit in the pace car – a highly modified saloon car – driven by one of the chief marshals who knew the circuit like the back of his hand. It was one of the most exhilarating experiences of my life – the famous mountain circuit sweeps up a long bending climb and then narrows, with walls close on each side, as it goes over the top. There is then the most incredible high speed, twisting descent, like the biggest, baddest rollercoaster you can ever imagine. It was an absolute buzz and I was still grinning like a Cheshire cat when I arrived back at the Morgan camp. I sat and had a coffee with Keith Ahlers, raving about my recent experience. 'Now I understand why you do it,' I grinned.

The forecast for race day was rain. I had heard rumours of legendary rainfall at the mountain circuit, but thought little of it. We had seen rain at Spa and apart from tropical downpours in South East Asia, I had never seen rain worse than that. The first storm hit during the morning, with still a few hours before race time. It was quite incredible. A dark, menacing cloud rumbled up very quickly, seemingly out of nowhere and simply dumped millions of gallons of water on the circuit. It was not so much rain as a waterfall from the sky. It continued for perhaps 15 minutes, then was gone as quickly as it had appeared.

I checked the forecast again. It predicted 'heavy showers' throughout the race period. One of the locals kindly showed me where to find an Australian government web site which carried live, real time weather radar. I set this up to give me a thirty-mile radius from the circuit and watched in fascination as it tracked storms approaching us. It was like a complex computer game; the worst storms showed up yellow with bright red in their core and I could see them heading in at quite a speed. Some veered off right or left at almost the last minute – a symptom of the mountainous terrain around us. Others came straight in. I tested the system with a real storm; and sure enough, I was able accurately to predict another massive downpour 15 minutes before it hit. Now I had something useful to do during the long hours of the race, in between the periodical reports to the media centre. Thankfully, it would also keep me out of the increasingly fraught politics in the camp.

The race started dry, but was very wet indeed within the first hour. I was able to give the pit garage an accurate 10-minute warning that rain was imminent, so they could prepare for the change to wet tyres in good time. The car seemed to be going pretty well, considering the appalling conditions. 'You make sure you don't get any Porsches up your backside!' I joked with Neil before his session. He gave me one of his disarming, boyish smiles, but he knew there was a serious point behind my jest, too.

The car came in with its first problem after a couple of hours. The engine was overheating and quite a lot of time was lost in the pit garage as the rag-tag team struggled to fix it quickly. There were only two mechanics – one from Richard Thorne's team and the other Keith Ahlers' – who knew the Morgan at all well. I had tried and failed several times to get Robert to understand that the car was very far from being run-of-the-mill. Its whole construction was unique and no mechanic, not even one as capable and adaptable as Darrell, could simply walk up and work on it effectively. I watched from a discreet distance. The problem seemed to be a bottom hose on the radiator –a particularly difficult job. The guys worked very hard – there was certainly no lack of enthusiasm and determination. Eventually, they got it back out.

The race was stopped soon afterwards during a particularly heavy downpour that turned the track into a river within seconds. There was nothing to do but wait. Things settled down again for a while and each of the four drivers had

Above and opposite: The Aero 8 handles well in the torrential rain at Bathurst. (Melissa Warren)

the chance to put in a stint. They were all doing an incredible job in the awful conditions. Calamity struck about 6 hours into the race. I was in the pits and saw the car flash by down the pit straight. Just out of sight, at the end of the straight, there was a loud bang and a big cloud of smoke. The engine had blown; a con rod piercing the wall of the engine. The team tried valiantly to recover, but it was all over. My worst fears – that the Cup car was simply not suited for an endurance race – had sadly come to pass. It was a sad end to a valiant effort. But I did not think it had had been a disaster. The warm welcome and attention we had received from the Australian fans had been remarkable and I was very pleased with the media coverage. I had also been able to manage things so that a clear distinction was understood between the Cup car and the Morgan Works Team proper. I had had a good opportunity to watch the way Robert worked and learned some important things that I stored away for later reference.

Later that night, we gathered around a TV screen in the camp and watched England win a famous victory over the Aussies in the rugby world cup final, accompanied by much drinking. It was great compensation for the English contingent, but something of a double whammy for Darrell and his Aussie boys. They took it very well.

Waking with a bad hangover the next day, I felt I had had more than enough of the claustrophobia of the race team. There were a couple of days free until our flight back and I wanted badly to break free and steer my own ship. I took the first available lift back to Sydney, checked into a very good hotel and played at being a tourist in that wonderful city until it was time to leave.

fourteen

Home of the Brave

Back home, Christmas was looming and so were some important decisions. I had long discussions with Robert every day about the way forward. There was absolutely no doubt in my mind that if we were going to get our Le Mans entry, we had to go to Sebring. It would not be a cheap exercise.

Immediately after Christmas, I travelled again, this time to Los Angeles, where Morgan was launching the new, American-specified Aero 8 road car at the LA Motorshow. Tom Hollfelder kindly agreed to bring along one of his racing Cup Class cars and Adam Sharpe flew in to add further weight to the racing story. The show was a big success on all levels. Our master plan, which included using the forthcoming Sebring race to give momentum to the road car launch in the USA, looked like being a winner.

Back home, efforts to get sponsorship continued apace and I had one important success. Yokohama, the Japanese tyre company, were very interested in our activities and with help from Mark Aston at the Morgan factory, we secured a deal for them to provide us tyres free of charge and technical support for a programme including Sebring, the Le Mans test weekend and the big race itself. This was very significant support, adding up to tens of thousands of pounds value. So our tyre costs were covered. But no matter how hard we tried, how many doors we knocked upon, we simply could not get a major cash sponsor. I did the budgets and I couldn't see how it was going to be possible.

Commercially, nothing had happened between Robert and I since the brief business conversation we had held after the Bugatti race in France. The Morgan Works entity had not been formalised, but Robert insisted on taking the role of 'Commercial Director', with sole responsibility for handling all monies – in and out. I had no problem with this: I was grateful to have a major management area covered. There was enough to do, on all fronts. Later I realised that the primary driver in Robert's approach was to ensure that he had a total grip on the spending of any money – either his own, or the team's.

The turning point in the Sebring discussions was eventually provided by Keith Ahlers. I had held various discussions with Keith about his ambitions to drive at

Le Mans with Morgan and we had met up in January at the motorsport show in Birmingham. I explained the commercial role that Robert was now playing and suggested that Keith talk to Robert about a drive at Sebring, with the promise of a seat at Le Mans should we succeed in getting the elusive entry. A deal was struck. We had a little cash flow and we were on our way to the USA.

Robert's determination to spend 'his' – and now 'our' – money without reference to me or anyone else soon produced a minor disaster. He booked a batch of very cheap flights and emailed the details to me. When I sent them on to the team, they quickly pointed out that the timings were simply unworkable; there would be no time to prepare the car for scrutineering on arrival and we would have to leave the circuit immediately after the race in order to catch the flight back – there would be not time to pack up, let alone rest.

I raised the issue with Robert, who was simply not prepared to discuss it. The cheapest flights, as ever, were not flexible. They were booked and paid for and that was that. 'The logistics people will have to prepare the car for scrutineering – that's it.' This seemed a completely crazy suggestion that finally confirmed to me that my worst suspicions were justified. The team was showing real signs of mutiny. There was little choice. I booked a new set of flights and paid for them with my own credit card.

That gut feeling I had experienced on arrival in Sydney – of not having full control of my destiny – was now beginning to be with me all the time, gnawing away in the background. Having grabbed back the essential US travel arrangements as a matter of necessity, I was forced to leave all other major logistical arrangements to Robert. To my mind, he had demonstrated several times now that he knew very little – and probably cared less – about the practicalities of running an endurance race team. I was seriously worried about the potential for real damage stemming from his single-minded crusade to cut costs to the bone.

It is relevant and fair to say that we were taking on impossible goals with very little funding and strict prudence was essential if we were going to get to our final destination. The concept of strict cost-cutting was far from alien to me. I welcomed it and the involvement of someone else to manage it. What gave real cause for concern was the unilateral application of the policy, without reference to its consequences.

Hence we arrived, tired and jetlagged, at Orlando on the rebooked flight. We proceeded to the car hire hall, to find a very long and slow moving queue at the counter for the budget rental company with which Robert had pre-booked cars for us. We had already decided we would need to change the booking, as the small cars he had booked were not going to work for all the kit and personnel we would have to carry in and out of the circuit every day.

The queue was interminable. I noticed that the desk of a rival company next door was virtually free of people waiting, so I went over and asked if they had a suitable big people mover. They did and a few minutes later we were on our way, with another large dent showing on my credit card.

As we waited in the line, I received a text message from Robert. 'Great news!' it read. 'Darrell and a mate are flying in from Australia tomorrow to join us.' Much as I had liked and respected Darrell at Bathurst, I was far from pleased to get this news. The Works Team functioned in its own unique way; a delicate balance between some of the strongest characters I had ever met. I was not at all sure how the addition of another powerful character, plus another completely unknown one, would be received. And more, I was less than enamoured by the lack of discussion and the clear implication, once again, that Robert needed his 'own man' in the camp to look after his interests.

It was very late when we found the hotel. The bar was long closed and there was no food to be had. We asked how long was the drive to the Sebring Circuit and were told to expect a 90-minute journey. It was not a very happy team that hit the sack that night.

The gloom was not lifted the next morning, when we met in the breakfast room at six in the morning. The food was strange and uninviting and the coffee was simply appalling. We did not linger long. It was a featureless, long drive to Sebring down an anonymous American highway. This was mid-Florida and we passed continuous evidence of its twin industries – oranges and old age. Interspersed with endless orange groves were huge retirement estates, surrounded by their essential support systems; plastic surgeons, eye specialists, electric wheelchair manufacturers and of course, every possible requirement for a life of golf. It all seemed to add to a general feeling of mild depression that even the Florida sunshine could not lift. We finally arrived at the famous circuit and spent a couple of hours negotiating the esoteric bureaucracy of gate security. Previously, I had been shocked and amazed by the complex paper knots that had been tied by race officialdom in Europe. But this was a paper trail of a completely higher order. Never was the old jibe about 'Two nations separated by a common language' more true. I can honestly report that I had more difficulty comprehending the processes here than I had ever done in Belgium or France.

When we did get clearance for everyone, we set off through the vast paddock area to find our camp, hopefully set up already by Robert's advance party. We did not know what to expect. It did not take us very long to find the lowliest, grubbiest stand in the paddock. A half-finished tent, which had perhaps once been white, flapped forlornly in the breeze next to a 40ft transporter that looked like a veteran of a couple of major war zones. The car, which was venerated by those in the team more highly than most humans they knew, was a sad and slightly shocking sight, covered in travel dust and dumped unceremoniously on the concrete floor of the tent. We sat down, lit cigarettes and opened cans of coke. 'Well, gentlemen,' I said. 'Welcome to the glamorous world of international motorsport.'

Work was the only thing that was going to help. There was plenty to be done and the team set to organising the tent into some kind of imitation of a pit garage and assessing the state of the car. There was clearly not much heart in it all, so after a couple of hours I called a halt. 'Brunch?' I asked, and we were soon back in the minibus, heading for a diner we had spotted back on the highway.

It's said that an army marches on its stomach. In my humble experience, it is virtually impossible to get a race team to walk anywhere. But give them a decent feed and they will certainly work like Trojans. Revived by a huge intake of bacon, eggs, toast and gallons of coffee, it was a different bunch of Brits who headed back to work for the afternoon. The truck was unloaded, the pits set up, the car polished. By the end of a hot afternoon, the place almost looked reasonable. As the sun went down, we called it a day and started the long drive back up to the hotel. There was just time for the quickest of showers and to make it – before it closed at nine o'clock – to a restaurant across the way, where we met up with Robert, Neil, Adam and Keith Ahlers, who was again travelling with his wife, Sue. I had last seen them on that fateful night in Australia and it was good to see them again.

Next morning there was a unanimous decision to skip the hotel breakfast and head instead straight for the Sebring diner, next to the circuit. We were joined by Darrell and his mate, a quiet young Aussie the size of a small house. The banter between the guys was good. I hoped it would continue. An abiding memory from the diner was the orange juice. Here we were, sitting among millions of acres of orange groves. But the diner had no fresh orange juice – only concentrate.

After the Bugatti race, just a few weeks before, the car had been back to its home in Malvern, where it had been stripped down, examined for wear and tear and then reassembled after a deep maintenance programme to prepare it for the gruelling 12-hour race ahead. The concrete surface at Sebring, an old air force base, is notorious for its huge bumps and cracks. The perceived wisdom of many people I had spoken with was that 12 hours racing at Sebring was actually far tougher on the car than 24 on the much smoother circuit at Le Mans.

So the preparation had been deep and intensive, leaving nothing unchecked. However, nothing at all had been changed on the car, either exteriorly or with internal components; in other words, the car was exactly the same as the one that had sailed smoothly through the French scrutineering authorities. What's more, we were quite certain that the American authorities would reflect the undoubtedly warm welcome the American motorsport fans were going to give the Morgan. I am sure this was the cause of the quiet confidence that characterised our preparations for scrutineering. There was little to do on the car except to polish and repolish her.

The Sebring race is run under licence from the French ACO authorities as part of the 'American Le Mans Series'. This means that the event is subject to the same sporting regulations under which we had raced at the Bugatti circuit; the same rules that we hoped we would have to race under at Le Mans itself. This effectively makes the French authorities the senior party and indeed we were pleased to meet two senior and familiar faces from the French technical authorities as we waited for our turn in the scrutineering tent. They were there to oversee things and ensure that the ACO's status prevailed.

Somebody had apparently forgotten to explain these niceties to the local American officials. In the post 9/11 world, all Americans had become more insular and paranoid than ever before and one of the unfortunate side effects was that some Americans considered the French to be only slightly less loathsome that Osama Bin Laden himself.

It should be remembered that this was at the time when restaurants all over the USA were renaming 'French Fries' as 'Freedom Fries' in protest against France's stand against the invasion of Iraq. Here in the redneck south, it was quite plain that they were in no mood to take any crap from 'Cheese eating surrender monkeys'. I wondered if our British credibility, as one of America's few allies in the war, would produce a positive result for us. I did not have long to wait to find out.

The trouble began on the weighing scales. The rules under which we raced were based upon a total car weight to engine size/air intake restriction formula, designed to produce a level playing field. The engineering trick here is to keep the car's weight extremely close to the minimum permissible level in the category, but without going under the limit.

Weight, unlike many other technical issues, had never been a problem for the Morgan. The car had been well within the limits at the Bugatti race. Nothing had changed on the car. We did not give the subject a moment's thought…until the scales showed we were around 20kg under the minimum weight for our class. This simply could not be true. We asked for a re-weigh. The result was the same. Tension rose inside the hot, sticky tent. I quietly explained to the officials that the car had not changed since France. 'You're not in fucking France now, boy. You're in the US of A and ah'm telling you your car is too fucking light. Is that clear?'

There was no arguing with this. However, Darrell, who had been watching from the peripheral, clearly thought there was. He jumped onto the scales, his not inconsiderable weight sending the dial soaring. He started to bounce up and down on the scales. 'Something's not right here,' he said aloud, to no one in particular. Now I was really concerned. Whatever was right or wrong about the measurement, starting a fight with the American officials right at the start of scrutineering was not going to help us one bit.

The weight decision, if indeed it stood, would mean we would have to carry ballast to make up the required weight. This was annoying, but hardly mission critical. The mission was to get an entry to Le Mans, not win a point with scrutineers, no matter how out of order they might be. In any case, Darrell really had no right to be in there at all. I asked him to leave. Grudgingly, he retreated, but not very far. Things did not improve as we went through the various stages of scrutineering. At Le Mans, they used a number of specially

Body language; the American scrutineers looking for problems with the Aero 8. (David Dowse)

designed rigs to measure body panels, wing heights, shape and so on. At Sebring, these measurements were all done by hand and by eye. After a while, we simply stopped complaining and pointing out that the car had sailed through scrutineering before. It was quite clear that they were fixed on having a field day with us. So much for the 'friendly British' effect.

At the end of a gruelling, frustrating 3 hours, we had a long list of work from the scrutineers. The team estimated it would take 18 hours to complete and we were desperately short of equipment and tools. We were also desperately short of water, drinks and food. There had been no sign of Robert and the drivers all day and on this occasion Robert had won the argument about catering – he was to provide it himself. There were no catering facilities open anywhere on the site.

Just as I was planning to take a long trip outside to get essential food and drink, an American visitor called in to introduce himself. 'Hi David, I'm Jack Payne.' He grinned. Jack was the editor of a web magazine, racinglines.com, and he had been bitten by the Morgan Works story. He had given us some great coverage and in return I had promised him some space on the car to promote his site. We chatted briefly, but he could see the pit garage was now frantically busy as the team got to grips with the work from scrutineering. 'Anything you guys need?' he asked as he prepared to leave.

An hour or so later, Jack was back in his pick-up truck, which was loaded with water, soft drinks, beer and snacks. He had even bought two huge ice boxes and they were packed full of ice. We loaded it all into the back of the tent. I was blown away by his kindness in going to all that trouble. 'How much do I owe you, Jack?' I asked. He wouldn't take a cent. 'I'll be back in the morning to see if you guys need anything else. Here's my cell phone number. Just call me if I can help with anything.'

I can't explain how encouraging it was to receive this kind of support. We were down, under pressure and totally under-resourced. But out there, there were people who cared, people who were genuinely touched by our campaign and what it stood for. For me, Jack's kindness was a timely reminder of why I was here at all. It also shone a bright, revealing light on what was increasingly becoming a serious split at the top in the Morgan camp. In some ways, the whole Morgan Works Team journey had become a kind of metaphor for life and there were occasions when it threw me into deep contemplation. It seemed that whenever our motivation was clear and pure – in our case, true to the 'Morgan Way', we received enormous goodwill and assistance on our journey. But when other motives – ego, money, fame – crept into the equation, all that ever resulted was negativity and difficulty.

Apart from the trouble in scrutineering, my initial fears about Darrell's involvement were soon to be proved wrong. True, he was very much Robert's man. Just like at Bathurst, he seemed to have some kind of a budget agreed with Robert, though I never knew what it was or what it was supposed to cover. What was clear was that once again, Darrell's only hope of making any margin was to nail every cost down to an absolute minimum.

We needed a huge range of equipment to complete the required work and run the race. We were also short a number of people to run vital aspects like refuelling and fire control. Darrell set about sourcing everything we needed and he was incredibly effective. He was everywhere in the paddock, making friends, borrowing kit and sussing out people for possible work on the team. Every hour or so, he would arrive back at the camp, clutching a tool of some kind. The team worked flat out through the afternoon and into the evening. Robert arrived at one point with some pizza and soon disappeared again.

Our next visitor of note was Tom Hollfelder, the California-based Morgan racer who had been the first customer for Christopher's Cup Class Aero 8 race car. At the LA show, before Robert had effectively taken personal control of the logistics for Sebring, I had been negotiating with Tom to provide us with the infrastructure and personnel we needed. When Robert took over the negotiations, they had been unable to agree a deal and Tom was here with his own team taking part in one of the support races. It was typical of Tom's innately kind nature that, despite the failure of the commercial discussions, he had called by anyway to offer us the free loan of various kit. Darrell was delighted to meet Tom and was soon deep in discussion with him about various equipment he had

Midnight Cowboys: the Morgan Works Team works long into the Florida night to sort out the scrutineering list. (David Dowse)

been unable to find elsewhere. Another friend of Morgan had come along to help the cause when he was needed most.

We worked long into the night, leaving the circuit towards eleven that night to face the long slog up the highway. The team were determined to find a beer, despite the lateness of the hour. When we arrived at the hotel some time after midnight, we drove past it to a low, anonymous concrete building Bradders had spotted the night before. There were no windows and the single heavy door reminded me of a cell block, but inside the lights were burning, the juke box was loud and the beer was flowing. The locals gave us a real cowboy welcome.

We left the bar when it closed at two, all quite merry apart from whoever it was that had been voted the driver. The drive to the hotel car park was only about 500 meters. We parked in the vast, empty car park and everyone jumped out. Bradders and Mark Baldwin were soon searching in the boot (that's the trunk for our American friends) for their kit bags. From nowhere, a big car screeched up behind us. A figure jumped out. It was a cop. And he was very nervous. His hand was actually on the handle of his handgun, though he had not yet drawn it.

'Bradders, Mark, come out of there, now!' I hissed, hoping to God that the cop would not get too jumpy.

'What are you doing here?' The officer was very officious.

I tired to be diplomatic. 'We've been working very late at the Sebring race track, officer.' I said. 'This is our hotel and we're just trying to find our bags from the car.'

'Have you been drinking?' It was more of an accusation than a question.

I looked at the policeman. He seemed not much older than eighteen. 'Yes, sir, we had a beer on the way home.' He had carefully looked us all over now and seemed slightly more relaxed now he had heard we were British and we didn't seem to be armed.

'Well, y'all go straight to bed now, y'hear? And next time, you be sure to take it slow when you're driving into the parking lot.'

'Yes, of course. We will, officer, we will. Thank you. Good night.'

I think we all realised that we could very easily have been in deep trouble. The incident reminded me of just how foreign a country we were in and how much fear and paranoia was endemic in American society. I was very grateful to safely reach my room and that night I made doubly sure that the substantial room locks were set.

We were up and on the road again a few short hours later. Today would be critical. First, the hoped-for sign off by the scrutineers after all the hard work the team had put in to meet their requirements. Then, in the afternoon, the first free practice and qualifying sessions on the track.

The crowds were beginning to build and we began to see evidence of the legendarily mad crowds that flock to the Sebring event in huge numbers. On the now familiar highway down to the circuit, we passed massive motorhomes, some the size of the big race trucks themselves, some of them pulling vast trailers, as if even the biggest possible motorhome was still inadequate for a weekend at the race. For the first time, on this morning we had to queue to access the circuit, which raised an issue I was going to have to address before race day was with us. With a drive of 90 minutes to reach the track from the hotel, plus an unknown time in endless jams trying to get in to the circuit on race day, we would have to leave the hotel at half past four in the morning; and this after leaving the circuit well after midnight the night before following qualifying. It was clearly crazy to go back there.

But the perceived wisdom was that every hotel room for fifty miles around the circuit was booked up months in advance – mostly by speculators who would hold out for inflated prices. This of course was why we were billeted so far away. I decided to ask our good friend Jack Payne if he had any ideas. But first, we had to get our ticket to race from the scrutineers. They seemed a good deal more friendly this time, but we were still stuck on a problem with an alleged overhang of the body panels. The rules say that the wheels must not protrude over the outside edge of the body panels. Because of the Aero 8's peculiar curves, which bent in every direction, it was very difficult to assess this rule objectively on our car. The official were trying to do so by the simple expedient of looking vertically down over the wheel arch and closing one eye. Several individual scrutineers tried this entirely subjective 'test' in succession, then huddled together for a discussion. The boss turned to us and shook his head.

This was ludicrous. The test was clearly subjective and the results borderline. And in any case, we were arguing over what was at most a 2mm 'overhang', which could not possibly affect the performance of the car. We argued fruitlessly. I appealed to our French friends from the ACO, who watched from a corner. They shrugged their shoulders, powerless. The solution was provided by Keith Ahlers.

Keith had been watching the debacle from a short distance and his patience had finally expired. He went up to the car and literally attacked the questionable wheel arch with his bare hands, easily managing to bend the aluminium panel outwards. Horrible cracks appeared where the wheel arch joined the main body. 'There,' he said. 'Now tell me it overhangs!'

The ticket to race was issued.

As this was the first day of action on the track, the crowds were building fast. Among them were many Morgan fans, who had made the long trip from all over the USA to witness Morgan's first ever run in an American international race event. They established a camp in a grassy area next to the paddock, where they proudly parked up their gleaming Morgans and raised the Union Jack alongside the Stars and Stripes. By now there was a constant stream of excited visitors to our garage tent; some the result of the pre-race publicity coverage, some who were keen Morgan fans, others who just happened by. As usual, the combination of the car's unique look, our obvious relative poverty and our open, good-humoured response to visitors was a big hit. Memorable comments ranged from 'I can't believe you guys are actually here!' to 'Wow, what *is* that thing?' and 'Gee, so that's the wooden car, right?'

The Morgan aficionados apart, the general race crowd was very different here than I had experienced in Europe and Australia. Hell bent on a 'good time', they came loaded with dozens of cases of beer and every comfort imaginable. Out in the camp sites, there were incredible sights to be seen. Circles of trucks, reminiscent of those schoolboy Cowboy and Indian movies, formed encampments inside which were huge fires, arrays of sofas and armchairs, massive barbeque ranges, refrigerators and sound systems. Some even had large screen satellite TV rigged up, making the whole scene look like some weird drive-in movie. It was an incredibly macho world. The men were big, tough, tattooed and generally sported long moustaches and beards. The women – and there were a lot of them – were almost exclusively buxom, blonde and wild. Their uniform was a bikini top, hot pants or bikini bottoms, baseball cap and a collection of cheap, gaudy necklaces. I soon learned that they earned these trinkets in return for frequent flashes of their ample breasts as they rode around the circuit on special wooden platforms built high up on the back of pick-up trucks. The

Sebring race fans. (David Dowse)

girls with the most necklaces gained extra status. It was the wild west come to life. These fans, who generally seemed good-humoured despite their wildness, seemed puzzled by the Morgan. They had never heard of it. Most had never heard of England, either.

I had some sport talking to these people at the garage. 'Hot damn!' they would say. 'How fast does that thing go, man?'

'Where we come from,' I would reply, 'It's not how fast you do it that matters, it's how long you do it for!' 'Yeee Haaa! We'll drink to that!' And off they went to the next part of the show.

At some point, I knew that the boys were going to want to cut loose and get among the madness of the parties that were already in full swing. But first, we had work to do. Final preparations were being made for the car's first practice run. This was to be our maiden race with our new tyre partners, Yokohama. They gave us fantastic support from the outset, which itself added an amusing aspect to our general poverty. We had all the tyres we would ever need, for any condition and we had some of the world's top tyre technologists working with us. But we had no equipment for transporting tyres around the paddock, so they had to be rolled from the Yokohama camp to our paddock tent. Thankfully, it was only a couple of hundred yards away.

With the scrutineering nightmare finally over, it was time for me to concentrate on PR matters. I spent a couple of hours arranging photo shoots with the car and the team – firstly with our highly valued sponsors, Yokohama, and secondly with the Morgan supporters' clubs. They had made such a superb effort that I wanted to give them something back. We arranged that we would take the car over to their camp after the track session. I have never seen a more delighted bunch of people.

Practice and qualifying came and went without incident. The car was running smoothly, and the new tyres were well accepted by all the drivers. The times were perfectly adequate and a certain relaxed feeling descended on the camp. We had fun with the photo shoots, got the car back to the tent and then, as predicted, it was time to let the boys out to play for a while. I handed over the keys to our golf buggy and gave strict instruction for them to be no longer than an hour. I knew that this would be completely ignored. I was left alone at the tent. Jack Payne called by for a chat and I explained our problem with race day and our hotel location. He understood immediately. 'I have one idea,' he said. 'Give me an hour.'

Apart from when the car had actually been running and a few meal times when he had brought in some take away food, Robert had been strangely absent from the camp, as had the drivers. This actually suited me and probably the team, too, quite well – it was much easier to get on with our work without too many people around. But there was a worrying lack of communication between Robert and myself and it was a shame that Adam missed out on many PR opportunities simply by not being there at the right time. As I sat there alone, I wondered if Robert preferred not to be seen too much around our poverty-stricken camp. More likely, he was off somewhere pursuing one of his many other agendas.

The Malvern boys came back a couple of hours later, mildly drunk, very happy and full of amazing anecdotes about their explorations out in the fans' campsites. The best featured an enormously obese, gun-toting cop who had apparently objected to their taking a bend on the golf buggy on two wheels.

'Ah doan care *whaat* race team you're on. It's too early for that horseshit! You stop that horseshittin' around. Y'hear?' Mark Baldwin's rendition of the Southern drawl accent was hilarious. This incident and the cop's outrage, was destined to become part of the team's mythical lexicon.

Jack returned, smiling. He had found a friend's house, no more than five miles from the circuit, which would be empty the night before race day. While the team cleared up the camp, accompanied by endless repeats of the meeting with the cop, I went off with Jack for a recce.

Jack was as good as his word. Within 15 minutes, I was sitting on the porch of a lakeside cabin, drinking a cold beer with Jack and his friend, who turned out to be a retired Miami police officer. The peaceful calm of the lake view in

A family affair – the Morgan Works race car lines up with some good company in the paddock at Sebring. (David Dowse)

Sebring driver line up. From left to right: Adam Sharpe, Neil Cunningham, Keith Ahlers. (David Dowse)

the evening sunshine was a perfect antidote for the madness of the circuit. With sofas included, there were enough beds for the core team. It was perfect. I did a cash deal with Jack's friend and we headed back to the circuit. Tomorrow night, we could move in here, get a good night's sleep and be at the circuit bright and early without a long drive and queues.

It had been a good day. We had a great steak dinner at a nearby restaurant recommended by Jack, then headed back to the hotel for a relatively early night.

The next day, the true extent of the wild west show that is Sebring really hit. The roads were choked with all kinds of huge trucks, piled high with cases of beer and people hell-bent on partying. Many of them were already well into their parties miles from the circuit, sound systems blaring as they sat in the traffic jams. Inside the circuit, the crowds were incredible and moving about the paddock was something of an entertaining nightmare. Many of the trucks that were arriving by the hundred were piled high with sofas and other furniture. I asked Jack Payne about this. 'Yeah, it's something of a tradition. They bring all this old stuff, party on it all weekend, then they make the biggest fire with it. The different camps of people all compete to make the most smoke and flames. You sure don't want to be over there come Sunday morning!' He pointed in the direction of the camp sites. 'It can get nasty.'

On track action at Sebring. (Melissa Warren)

We kept practice and qualifying running time to a minimum, following our usual strategy of conserving the car and especially the engine. So for most of us the day before race day was relatively quiet. I spent a lot of it just talking to hundreds of visitors and well-wishers. The car was polished and preened. One man, though, was far from relaxed. Darrell was keeping up an incredible work-rate as he rushed around the paddock trying to find all the items of the list we had given him – things we didn't have but were critically needed in the pit lane for the race. I found the following list in my notebook, but probably extra items were added by others.

EZ UP tent
Power leads
Lighting
TV monitor
Table, chairs
Boom for air line
Air-line connection converters
Trolley Jack
Extra air bottles
Gloves and goggles for six people
Fireman (with full fireproof kit)
Extra person for refuelling

Darrell's supreme effort and his eventual success in finding most of these items for free is something of a tribute to Robert's 'screw them down' policy. Darrell was under a double incentive; he knew that without these items we could not race and he probably wouldn't get paid. He also knew that if any item cost anything, it could only come from one place – his own pocket.

By the end of the day, he had secured most of what we needed and in doing so gained big respect from the Morgan people, including myself. The team now split into two as planned; the core team, Bradders, Mark Baldwin, Rogier and Billy (Keith Ahlers' chief mechanic who had joined us for this race) and myself headed off to the lakeside cabin, while the rest started the long drive back up to the hotel.

Sitting by the lakeside, with cold beers in hand, we were very relaxed and comfortable and I was pleased that the plan, with Jack's inspired help, had worked so well. I always had a firm belief that morale really matters in pressured situations and this wonderful chill out, followed by an early night and a good restful sleep, was just what the doctor ordered. I awoke at around six to the fantastic smell of fresh coffee. Jack, who was fast achieving the status of archangel in my eyes, was already up. In the kitchen, a huge pot of fresh coffee stood next to a home-made lemon cake and a big jug of fresh orange juice – the first we had seen in Florida. We wandered outside and down to the lake's edge with our coffee and lemon cake, watching the early morning mist flicker across the surface of the water. A few feet away from the bank where we stood, there was a ripple in the water.

'What's that?'

We looked closer. Something was looking back.

'It's an alligator!' Sure enough, the unmistakable, prehistoric eyes protruded just above the water and about a foot in front of them I could clearly see nostrils flexing. I did a quick mental calculation that told me the head was about eighteen inches long. I took a couple of steps back.

Bradders, being Bradders, stepped closer and peered at the creature. He threw it a piece of cake. Jaws full of teeth opened and snapped shut, an almost cartoon-like movement. Then the head started moving, quickly and purposefully, towards the shore. Whether the alligator wanted more lemon cake, or a piece of Bradders for an entrée, wasn't clear. 'Time to go, I reckon,' I said.

The plan worked sweetly. Fifteen minutes after leaving coffee, lemon cake, lake and alligator, we were in the garage tent at the circuit and the team was in remarkably high spirits. The car was checked, polished and tweaked in a relaxed fashion. A little later, Darrell and the others arrived and started gathering together our rag-bag of pit lane paraphernalia and assembling it down at trackside. Darrell had done a fine job of acquisition and several other teams, Tom Hollfelder's in particular, had been very generous in lending equipment. By the time the tent was up, lights were connected and TV screens on, it almost looked like a proper race team set up.

The pit stop that Darrell made; begged and borrowed kit on the front line with Morgan Works. (David Dowse)

We were at Sebring for one reason only; it was an essential stepping stone to the elusive Le Mans entry. The race itself was relatively unimportant, so long as we did not disgrace ourselves. Watching the car disappear into the first turn after the start, I felt a huge sense of relief. Just starting the 12-hour event represented another tick on my slowly reducing list of tick boxes. The effort and stress of getting to this point had been intense, but now it felt good. She was running.

And she was running very well indeed. The hours came and went. Scheduled pit stop followed scheduled pit stop. Drivers changed smoothly, each of them doing a sterling job keeping things running like clockwork and avoiding all trouble. The new Yokohama tyres were performing superbly, giving us full double sessions before needing changes. Time in the pits was minimal. Finally, we had come together. There was little to do in the pits, other than pray for a continuing quiet life. Hours went by. Darkness fell. The Aero 8 came in for one unscheduled pit stop – for a blown headlight bulb. And that was it. As the chequered flag approached, Morgan fans gathered behind the chain link fence that separated the pit lane from

Fingers crossed by everyone in the pit lane as the Aero 8 marches on at Sebring. (David Dowse)

Sebring pit stop action. twelve hours racing, fuel, tyres, driver changes – and a headlight bulb required. (David Dowse)

the public area. They were all grinning from ear to ear. The noise made it quite impossible to speak with them, but I am sure my 'thumbs up' and 'fingers crossed' said everything that was needed at that moment. The special roar of the Morgan's twin side pipes blasted by for the last time and I remember screaming 'Yes, yes, yes!' at the top of my voice, thankfully drowned out by the noise from the track.

I raced off to get the official results from the press room. With very little money, borrowed equipment and stacks of goodwill from the fans behind us, we had just finished one of the toughest endurance races in the world in tenth position of twenty-two GT class entries and twentieth position overall of a field of forty-four starters. We had beaten both TVR entries and several of the Porsches. We had quite definitely arrived. It was a very good feeling indeed.

We had now ticked every major box on the list I had written down almost a year before, after the massive blow of the refused entry. The Le Mans entry list

Neil Cunningham storms on into the night and into the record books, booking our place at Le Mans with the first Morgan run at the Sebring 12 Hour race. (Melissa Warren)

was due to be published a few days after our return from the USA. I felt a strange calm about the situation now; I was still by no means certain that we would get our entry, but I was absolutely clear in my heart that, together with the whole team, I had done everything possible to secure it. If we failed now, I felt I could give up the quest and still hold my head up.

When it finally came, the decision was something of an anti-climax. Having famously received a fax letter informing us of our failure in 2003, I expected a fax to confirm our success this time. No fax arrived. The entry list was simply published at a given time. And there, towards the end of the long list of Porsche and Ferrari entries in LM GT class, were the words that had taken over a year of blood, sweat and tears to achieve: Morgan Works Team, Aero 8 LMGT. We had won the right to finish our business at Le Mans.

fifteen

Testing times II

Any feeling of euphoria was very short-lived. There was now another long succession of bridges to cross and mountains to climb before we could get to the starting grid in June. First, we would have to go to the compulsory Le Mans test weekend in April and get all three of our drivers qualified there. In logistical terms, this event is almost as complex – and as costly – as the race itself. The car needed many hours of work to assess wear and tear from Sebring and prepare it for the test and the big race. We were going to need a major engine refresh and a whole load of spares. We would also have to commit soon to hotel bookings and travel arrangements for both the test weekend and the race itself. There was one further detail – we now had to confirm our acceptance of the entry invitation by sending a rather large cheque. Long, hard conversations with Robert now took place almost hourly and literally thousands of emails flew. The compulsory attendance at the test weekend caught him by surprise. Costs were mounting up and there was no major income in sight, save for potential payment from drivers. With the entry secured, I renewed our efforts to secure sponsorship.

One significant breakthrough came from this effort; thanks to a timely intervention by a Morgan fan employee, P&O Ferries agreed to cover all our cross-Channel transport requirements for both the test weekend and the race itself. This was a very welcome development and was worth tens of thousands of pounds. However, it made only a slight dent in the overall funding requirements. We needed a deal with a driver, a lucrative one. Adam Sharpe's place was secure following Robert's previous financial input and Adam's solid performances behind the wheel. Neil Cunningham's seat was rather more fragile; Neil, though by far our best driver, had no sponsorship funding and was not in a position to fund his drive as a privateer. The potential value of the drive was up to £40k and discussions with Robert were very intense. My position was unequivocal; Neil had been a essential and totally loyal player in the whole project and if there was any way it could be done, he absolutely must have the drive with Morgan Works at Le Mans. Robert's opinion of Neil was no lower than mine (save that naturally he would always put his son first), but Robert was much more of a realist. As

'Commercial Director' he was, of course, in charge of finances. We agreed that we would both look for possible paying customers for the third seat.

Keith Ahlers was the number one contender for both of us. Keith had done a solid job at Bathurst and Sebring and we had promised him first option on a Le Mans drive if we were successful with gaining the entry. Robert negotiated a deal with Keith to cover both the test weekend and the race. I was delighted. Keith had been a pleasure for me to work with, both in Australia and America, and he was a genuine 'Morgan man.' Cash-flow was fluid again. But we were now living and working each day at a time.

The next critical event was a meeting held at the Morgan factory soon after the entry announcement. The meeting was chaired by Morgan's new executive chairman, Alan Garnett, appointed after the death in late 2003 of Charles' long-serving and much loved father, Peter Morgan. We were joined by Charles Morgan; sales and marketing director, Matthew Parkin; finance director, Tim Whitworth; Steve Morris, who had recently been promoted to a well-deserved position on the Board as operations director; and Christopher Lawrence.

Alan Garnett expressed enthusiastic support for the project and thanked the whole team, through me, for their efforts in getting thus far. He went on to explain once more that it was impossible for the Morgan Motor Company to provide any cash funding for the project. However, he committed the factory to helping in every other way possible. The car would be made available to us at no cost, all Morgan OE spares would be provided free of charge and the factory would also agree to release whatever personnel were required to run the car.

In the circumstances, this was a superb outcome. For the first time, I felt that we now had the whole Morgan 'family' behind us. Morgan Works could now truly represent the factory and its history – the things that had originally inspired its creation and had kept us going through all the adversity of the past year.

I had a follow-up meeting with David Bradley and Mark Baldwin to explain where we had got to. Mark now came up with a superb idea. 'If we are going to be a real Morgan Works Team,' he said, 'The car should be run by people from the Morgan factory.'

I completely agreed with his inspired thinking. There was nobody in the world who knew the Aero 8 as well as Mark's team in the factory service department and working around the factory there were other individuals who had invaluable specialist expertise. At a stroke, two major problems on my list had evaporated; staffing the team and paying their wages. So far as team management was concerned, it also kept the pecking order within the team clear and unequivocal – something that I had learned could be problematical when outsiders were brought in. I went home very pleased with the day's work.

We were still a very long way from being out of the woods. There remained a substantial difference between the detailed budget I had worked up and agreed with Robert and the projected income, even though large inroads had been made by the advent of Yokohama and P&O Ferries and the renewed background support from the Morgan factory. Every day, I would rack my brains to find a way to cover more of the costs. Among the big areas of expenditure that were left unsponsored were hotels and catering. I tried and failed to find a sponsor to cover these specific areas. We revived the concept of the 'Exclusive Partners' scheme, giving people much lower cost options to be involved in the team. Quite a few immediately responded with donations of £50, for which they would have their name on the car in the race. Every single pound and dollar counted.

At the workshop in Malvern, Rogier Vancamelbecke was working full time on stripping down the car after the trails of Sebring. We were delighted with its general condition. Even after such a gruelling test, the major repair to the rear end following the crash at Spa had held up perfectly; a real testament to the peerless fabrication work of Ben Coles. There was very little wear and tear on major componentry either – some minor wear damage to clutch and gear box parts, worn out wheel bearings – but nothing that should not have been expected. This was a great relief, not least because funding any new parts required was a real problem. Charles Morgan was working hard to arrange a deal with Mader that would hopefully resolve the very great chasm between our need for refreshed race engines and our ability to pay market rates for them.

Mark Baldwin, fired up by the factory's renewed interest in our activities and the central part that he and his own factory men would now play in it, was making good progress in hiring the race truck and certain key equipment we would need at a very advantageous rate. Mark was known and liked by many in the business and it looked like this was about to produce a substantial pay off. Every favour would be called in.

The hours, days and weeks raced by in a frenzy of activity and stress. Existing sponsors needed supporting and nurturing, their logos ordered and placements agreed. Potential new sponsors needed pressing. Hotels and transport had to be booked, vehicles hired, equipment borrowed. We were also very busy with the vital PR aspects of the project, keeping fans informed and trying to whip up more interest that might, even at this late stage, convert to funding. More than ever before, the campaign became an all-encompassing personal maelstrom, each day presenting a number of seemingly impossible problems to overcome. My credit cards were taking a very severe battering and so was my relationship with family and friends.

My relationship with Robert was also becoming strangely fraught for two people who were ostensibly partners working towards the same goal. Like me, he had a family and a business to run outside of the Morgan campaign. Unlike me, though, for Robert it was not a Morgan crusade. I don't believe he ever saw or felt the sheer love for the brand and what it represented, nor the goodwill that had carried us to this position in our impossible dream. This is not a criticism; it is simply an observation. In many ways, I believe I was seduced and at least part-blinded by the heady emotional story. Certainly I was completely single-minded, with a single topic of conversation. It must have been tough on those around me who did not feel driven the way I myself did.

With the availability of the extra hands from within the factory, this was the right moment to restructure things formally. Through all the ups and downs and personnel changes of the past year, a solid core had evolved. David Bradley, who had begun life with the 2002 campaign as electronics expert and liaison person with engine suppliers Mader, had been with us throughout and had grown to fit bigger shoes. He was now 'officially' made technical manager. Bradders would also run the 'front of car' operations during the race. Mark Baldwin, solid as the Rock of Gibraltar, would have his own house team working under him and was the only possible choice for chief m echanic. Rogier 'the cabin boy' Vancamelbecke, who had so diligently managed the car build since Steve Lawrence's departure, became a race mechanic. He was to be joined by John Burbidge, who had by now done his time in penance for the violent outburst in the team minibus back in January 2003 and was rehabilitated to the prestigious Development Team at the factory. We would also be able to call upon the expertise of our seconded Yokohama tyre specialist Ian Beverdige, Lutz Passon from suspension partners KW and data analysis specialist Mick Boasman. Working under Bradders and Mark Baldwin would be a team of around twelve additional people drawn from the factory staff.

It was the strongest and most cohesive team we had ever fielded and with the exception of the outside specialists, who had effectively already been welded into the team proper, it was now a truly Morgan affair.

As we prepared once again for action in the paddock at Le Mans, I had my usual few minutes of reflection. I strolled up the hill to where I could look down on the paddock area and sat quietly, pondering everything that had transpired during the past eighteen months. The long, hard journey was nearly over. At least, the beginning of the end was in sight. Part of me felt that just having secured the entry was a victory in itself. But I was not unaware of what still lay in front of us.

After two very successful outings at the Bugatti Circuit race and in Sebring, the test weekend was to give us a strong warning about just how severely any sign of complacency or smugness would be treated. Looking back, it seems to me that the press bulletin I issued immediately after the weekend tells the story quite well. Here it is in full:

28 April 2004 – immediate release.

The Morgan Works Team finished a gruelling day at Le Mans on Sunday with mixed fortunes. Adam Sharpe and Neil Cunningham completed the required 10 laps to qualify, but a dramatic series of events in the afternoon session prevented third driver Keith Ahlers from making the starting grid in June – despite the superhuman efforts of the pit crew.

Lining up together for the first time at the Le Mans test, April 2004 – the full, true Morgan Works Team. We later realised that the car was pointing the wrong way round the circuit! (David Dowse)

Mechanics from the Malvern factory hard at work preparing the car for the Le Mans test weekend. (David Dowse)

Testing times II

Following a faultless run in the 12 Hour race at Sebring just a few weeks ago, the team arrived at Le Mans for the vital pre-race test in confident mood.

The objectives were to qualify drivers Adam Sharpe, Neil Cunningham and Keith Ahlers by completing the required 10 laps each and then to carry out some development work in the afternoon session. The full technical team, including specialists from Yokohama, KW Suspension and Magnetti Marelli data management were in attendance to assist with this plan.

During the morning session, all went smoothly and on plan. Neil Cunningham handled the shake down laps perfectly and the Aero 8 LM GT steadily improved to a satisfactory lap time of 4.27. The outlook was good for an afternoon best lap time on target around 4.18.

Adam Sharpe took over at around 11.30 and put in 8 laps at a steady 4.35 pace as he learned the circuit; a superb performance from the 19 year old - the youngest of the 150 drivers at Le Mans in 2004.

As the lunch break approached, the team prepared for the planned change of differential that would commence the afternoon's development programme. Keith Ahlers was ready to complete all or most of his 10 laps before the break.

However, the best laid plans are notoriously subject to the vagaries of motorsport and the afternoon turned out to be a very different experience for the Works Team.

Just before the driver change, Adam came in with a steering problem, which turned out to be a blown seal on the rack. The team decided to end the session there and change both steering rack and differential over lunch. Adam still had 2 more laps to complete to make the required 10.

The work went smoothly and Adam was back out as soon as the circuit re-opened. 15 minutes later he was in for the change over to Keith. But on his very first lap, Keith broke down near Mulsanne with reported transmission failure. First indications were that the clutch had gone, which would have meant the game was prematurely over. The team towed the car back in and quickly found that the fault was actually a broken drive shaft, which was rapidly repaired. Keith was soon back out to big sighs of relief.

Then, after just one more flying lap, Keith suffered a bad crash going into the Porsche Curves and on the circuit monitors the car looked a complete write off. The Pit Marshalls actually signed the session closed for Morgan.

But once again, the team dragged the stricken car back in and worked frantically to repair serious damage to front and rear wings. The tow truck had sheared off the rear spoiler wing. Dispensation to run without it was urgently sought, as well as permission to re-open the test session. Time was fast running out and Keith still only had 4 laps on the board.

To cheers from the crew, the crowd and even the marshalls, the car went out again, held together with large amounts of tape and many prayers. But still the fates had not finished with Morgan Works. Another couple of laps in, Keith broke down again, this time with a broken front driver side wishbone - a consequential result of the early crash. Once again it looked like it was all over.

But the Morgan Works Team is famous for simply refusing to give up and now the large crowd was treated to a stunning demonstration of just how much spirit it has. The car was towed back in and the broken wishbone was welded up with the much-appreciated help of another team in the paddock. With just 9 minutes of the session left, the car was ready to roll again. The team's calculations had Keith requiring two more laps. In a heart-stopping development just as the car rolled out of the garage, the safety officials stopped the car, requiring some additional work to make the battered car safe.

The clock was ticking away. Finally, the Aero 8 roared off to more cheers and Keith Ahlers valiantly tried to complete the necessary laps. In the end, though, time and luck had run out and it was simply not possible to complete the last lap before the chequered flag ended the session, the day and Keith's hopes for a Le Mans drive in 2004.

The search must now commence for a driver who has pre-qualified by racing at Le Mans in the past.

Team Manager David Dowse comments:
'That was an incredible effort from the team and we are extremely disappointed that in the end we couldn't get Keith qualified. On the upside, though, the drivers reported that the car was handling beautifully during the morning session and we are completely confident that we can run at a pace that will put us somewhere in the centre of the class. Certainly our best time of the day is no indication of what the car is capable of doing – we simply didn't get the chance to put our foot down.'

Ends

There are a few details that we did not make public at that time. Firstly, during the white heat of that incredible afternoon, I had made what was possibly my biggest mistake so far in the campaign. When the pit marshals had handed me a form to sign following Keith's initial crash, I had signed it; the combination of the TV pictures I had seen myself and the track marshalls' reports convincing me that the crash was terminal. When Bradders and Mark Baldwin dragged the car back in and set about kicking and beating it back into shape, I had to run to the race office to try to reverse the decision to which I had just agreed. By pure fortune, I had bumped into the young Marshall concerned and with the timely help of some assistance with translation from Anne Morel, one of Robert's 'personal' French support team, we were able to persuade him to come back and reopen our book.

It was a mistake for which I was later to pay dearly.

The other issue concerns the situation with Keith Ahlers. When the session ended, it was pretty clear that Keith had not completed enough laps. However, the race authorities were due to publish the result of their deliberations a couple of hours after the track closed. The authorities have some discretion in this decision. Anne Morel, whose value to Robert as a consultant depended largely on her native speaking French and her close relationship with many of the senior race officials, went off to 'put in a good word' with anyone who would listen. Personally, I was a little doubtful about the value of this intervention.

Anne returned to tell us that a decision would be made and the results would be posted at the race office shortly. Robert and I went off on the golf buggy to

Keith Ahlers keeps a close eye on the monitors as he awaits his turn at the Le Mans test. Knockhill. (David Dowse)

wait for the vital document. We waited for a couple of hours. Nothing happened and no one could tell us when something might. It was getting late and we both had long drives back to England ahead of us. I set off back up to Le Havre, Robert promising to call me the moment any news broke.

A couple of hours later, an excited Anne Morel called me to say that Keith's name *was* on the official press list of approved drivers for the race. An hour later, after I had already called Keith to tell him the great news, Robert called to say it had been an error; he was looking at the list and it clearly did NOT include Keith's name; and this was definitive.

The calm and understanding way in which Keith accepted the content of my second phone call to him that evening proved to me that he is one of the few true gentlemen operating in international motorsport. The decision was confirmed by fax the following day, regretting that as Mr Ahlers had not completed the minimum number of laps, they were unable to confirm his acceptance. Now we had to find another driver, quickly. With some funding.

We also had a badly smashed car, new question marks over the reliability of key components, no budget available and just a few short weeks in which to resolve it all before the race proper. Thankfully, lady luck was still with us, although she did seem very reluctant to show her face at times. On closer examination at the factory, the damage to the car was limited to body panels and the wooden frame, both elements which the in-house experts at Malvern could repair quickly. That the car had been slammed into an unforgiving French concrete wall at high speed, but the chassis was unharmed, was yet another testimony to Christopher Lawrence's incredibly tough design and the inherent strength of the Morgan's wooden sub-frame structure.

Technically, at least, we were not in bad shape. Things were not so good in other departments. By now – it was May 2004 – I was very concerned indeed about the financial position. My credit cards were all creaking under the strain of keeping things afloat. The new Morgan Works Ltd company, mooted months before back at the Bugatti race, had never properly materialised, beyond the signing of some papers. Robert was, at least in theory, the 'Commercial Director', but I was still waiting for repayment of large amounts of expenses I had covered personally in Florida and at the test weekend. There were a great many more things that I knew would have to be paid for and I was very worried that either I would inevitably run out of credit and so be unable to cover something critical, or that I would never be repaid the money I was laying out. Or, quite possibly, both.

A team meeting was convened, during which Robert – quite unexpectedly – willingly agreed to my original suggestion of a small share issue to David Bradley, Mark Baldwin, Neil Cunningham and Adam Sharpe. It was a rapid conversion of position which perhaps should have rung more alarm bells. The meeting went on to consider our funding position. I made it clear that I was unable to continue paying out large sums to cover costs. In response to a direct question from Mark Baldwin, for his part Robert made it plain that ultimately, he personally, or via sponsorship from one or more of his business interests, would cover any shortfall between the budget requirements and the income. The project could go forward, though there had been no direct discussion or agreement about repayment of the money I had already committed. There was so much to do and so little time. I acquiesced, leaving the subject for a later discussion.

The rest of the meeting was taken up largely with one subject; that old chestnut, the catering. After the disappointment and let down at Bugatti and also after we had experienced Robert's DIY approach to feeding the team in Sebring and the Le Mans test, I was quite determined that we must have professional catering for the big race. Apart from the very real need to feed a large number of people regularly and well, the paddock catering facility is also part of the team's presentation. We must have somewhere to greet sponsors and guests and at least be able to offer them a seat and a drink.

The problem, of course, was the cost. Despite the Bugatti let down, my preference was still for the company that had looked after us so well at Spa. Both Robert and I had had words with the woman who ran the business and she can have been left in no doubt that we expected blue riband treatment; she owed us and more particularly, she owed me personally. Ever suspicious of any but his own negotiating powers, Robert had taken over and tried to beat down the original quote. He had failed to make much progress. Thankfully, Bradders and Mark were both strongly on my side in this heated discussion. Unlike Robert, they had seen the superb service that had been served up at Spa and they knew just how important food would be.

We now had a real impasse. Robert had now said on record that he would personally cover any budget shortfall. This effectively meant that he would have to pay for whatever catering we had. And he was quite adamant that he was not going to pay for our preferred choice. His wife Kerstin, helped by other members of the family, would look after the catering. 'And that's final,' he said.

It wasn't. The discussion went on. I explained how many meals were needed and how frequently they would need to be served. I explained that they would need to be hot meals, not just sandwiches. I explained the impossibility of getting in and out of the circuit to bring in supplies during race weekend. Robert would not be moved. Kerstin had to leave early. There was no more to be said. We had lost the argument. A few minutes after she had left, Robert got a text message and asked to be excused for a moment. He went outside, to return after a short while with a very strange expression on his face. It was a kind of smile, but somehow he did not seem at all amused.

'Kerstin has decided she doesn't want to do it. So you'll get what you want.'

The full import of the discussions at that meeting were not to become clear until after the race. However, there was one immediate and critical effect. For many months, I had been responsible for paying the wages of key people in the team. At times, this had been incredibly difficult, requiring the delicate juggling of my own personal and business resources and often having to find large sums in cash at short notice. Now I had simply run out of money. At the meeting, I had finally drawn a line under this and the individuals concerned would now invoice and be paid by Robert direct.

It is often said that 'He who pays the piper calls the tune...' Perhaps rather naively, I had thought that my long and close relationship with the individuals concerned and the way I had gone many miles extra to ensure they were always paid, would ensure that we did not see too much of this impact within the Morgan Works Team. Sadly, I was to be proved wrong.

For the time being, though, there was much to do and no time to dwell. The race was only a couple of weeks away and operations increased to fever pitch on all fronts.

The important issue of the third driver was eventually resolved, our old friend Steve Hyde stepping in at a late stage with just enough funding to make things work. After the initial conversation, I passed Steve directly to Robert for the two of them to conclude the business deal. With impeccable credentials from his 2002 Le Mans drive with the DeWalt Morgan Team, Steve was an ideal candidate.

A minor flurry of late individual supporters came in, bringing small but vital amounts of money – all of which was controlled by Robert's own office. By now I was feeling quite isolated, with no control or influence over commercial matters and very little meaningful dialogue with Robert. I did not consider this latter to be particularly sinister; we were both incredibly busy. If we were going to complete the task I had set for us eighteen months before, now was the time for total concentration and determination. There would be time for a sort out later.

sixteen

Breakdown

Finally and all too quickly, race week was upon us. Two years after the fateful 2002 event, we were on our way to Le Mans again. Though it seemed almost to have been going on all my life, it had been just twenty-four months of intense effort, extreme disappointments and impossible obstacles. Somehow, we had overcome almost all of them and here we were. It was a strange, dreamlike feeling as we made our way down the now familiar long road to Le Mans from the Channel ports.

Despite vigorous protest, Christopher was finally persuaded by a concerted effort from his wife Carey, myself and Charles that he should not travel to the race. We knew, as Christopher himself knew, that if he did so he would not be able to take it easy, to be a VIP guest. He would get on the pit wall and want to stay there all night, and his health was simply not up to it. Grudgingly, he gave in, consoled by the live 24-hour broadcast he could access on satellite.

Surprisingly, Charles announced that he himself would not be going either. Instead, it would be left to Alan Garnett, the company's new chairman, and a coach load of people from the factory, to fly the corporate flag.

The advance party consisted of myself, Bradders, Mark Baldwin, Rogier Vancamelbecke and Mark Davies, a solid workhorse I had brought in to help with the pit set up, electrics and to double as aide-de-camp. For once, we contrived to arrive on site in good time, so that we had the rare luxury of three relatively relaxed days to get everything ready for the arrival of the main body of the team later in the week. Even so, when we pulled into the paddock, many of the bigger teams were already well entrenched, some of them building major structures in and around their pit garage.

After I had paid the cash deposit to pick up the key to our allocated garage, we wandered down the line of trucks to find our place. Initially, we were disappointed. Our home for the next ten days was to be at the extreme end of the line, next to the pit lane exit, in one of the single-storey garages that had been specially added for the filming of the Steve McQueen Le Mans film in the 1970s. It was remote from the centre of activity and we felt like the poor relations who had been shoved away where they would not be noticed too much. Probably the fact that, in the company of the big Audi, Porsche and Ferrari teams we were quite literally the poor relations probably made us feel the inequity more keenly. But as we looked around more carefully, the situation began to improve. To our left, our immediate neighbours were one of the Audi teams, who were busy building a virtual village at the back of their garages. Their construction work was substantial, even incorporating parts of the permanent grandstand structure. I marvelled at the incredible degree of forethought and planning that must have been involved. The crew were a friendly bunch – and they would certainly have every conceivable piece of kit available. It boded well for our inevitable borrowing missions.

On our right side were a couple of privately-funded French prototype teams. They were very down-to-earth and we were warmed by the sight of battered tool boxes just like our own. The marshalling area directly behind us widened here, so we were much less cramped than we would have been closer to the centre of the pit lane. Out front, we had a little space to the left, which would make pit stops much easier. There was a big grandstand directly opposite us and a permanent TV station on the pit wall just to our left. I realised then that with the front-running Audis right next door, the TV cameras would be constantly on them during their stops; we would be superbly placed to get 'piggy back' TV exposure. The guys had a look around, found toilets nearby, power supplies and water and pronounced themselves well satisfied. We had landed and we were happy with our lot.

Mark Baldwin soon had our truck in position and the long job of unloading began. The first major item to go in was the plastic flooring. A mandatory requirement, the flooring had already been quite a saga in its own right. With no budget to buy it, before we left England I had spent hours phoning round in a vain attempt to borrow some flooring from another team. Robert had solved the problem at the eleventh hour and the truck had diverted on its way down to pick up big rolls of black flooring from a farmer friend of his. As we unrolled it onto the hallowed ground of our Le Mans pit garage, good English grass, mud and the occasional piece of sheep shit revealed themselves stuck to the plastic tiles. After a few hours of pressure hosing and hand scrubbing, we decided it was as good as it was going to get. It seemed like the right moment to close the doors and head off for a late lunch and a siesta at the hotel.

The holiday was soon over. During the following two days the team put in long hours, fitting out the pit garage with interior walls, power, lighting, workbenches and toolkits. Bradders and Mark had dreamed up an outside lighting structure that would not have disgraced a stadium rock and roll band. Great sections of aluminium girders and steel tensioners were carefully erected and massive halogen lighting units hung from them. The job took all of a long, hot day to complete. As darkness fell, the lights were switched on for their first test, flooding the whole of our pit frontage with blinding light. It was far and away the brightest display in the whole of the pit lane. Bradders and Mark pronounced themselves very happy with their work.

Within a few seconds, millions of mosquitoes and midges were swarming around the brightest beacon in France, so many of them immolating in the fiery heat that an acrid smell filled the air. Those that survived soon found English blood very much to their taste. 'Better put mosquito cream on the shopping list,' said Bradders.

The people of Le Mans generally love the racing teams. This may be connected in some way to the estimated 200 million Euros that this one race injects into the local economy every year. Whatever their reasons, we enjoyed the warm welcome. During our previous visits to the world's greatest motor racing city, we had found some essential local resources; a bar near the circuit that was always still open in the small hours – when we often finished work; several small, cheap restaurants that were never phased by the arrival of twenty dirty, hungry men; bars near the station where several race teams would often gather at the end of the day.

The locals loved all the race teams, but many seemed to have a special place in their hearts for Morgan. They were well informed about our trials and tribulations, which was gratifying. 'Le Morgan! C'est le courage!' they said, pumping our hands. Naturally, we encouraged this goodwill and invested in it by judicious handing out of team caps, or for special friends, highly coveted T-shirts. When we weren't forthcoming, they would sometimes demand. On more than one occasion, team members left bars without their shirts. In one or two of our favourite haunts, we were well remembered from our previous visits and were greeted like family friends. The importance of this warmth and the very real kudos to be gained from wearing the team uniform should not be underestimated. These things are part of the ethereal compensation for all the graft, the pain and the anguish of endurance racing.

Morale was high. The hotel was not too far away, it was quiet and clean and the showers worked. We were eating well and often and there was time for a few drinks and banter at the end of the working day. The welcome was genuine and warm. The pit garage was coming on well. Tomorrow, the rest of the team would arrive from the factory. Scrutineering should be a walk in the park.

The days were fast counting down to race time and with the arrival of the team minibus and the catering truck things stepped up a gear. At the circuit, security was beginning to swing into action. This is one of the strangest aspects of working inside a race team at a world-class event like this. When you first arrive, often many days ahead of race day, things are pretty relaxed. The tempo and the level of activity gradually build – at first each day becoming a little busier, then accelerating by the hour until everything is at a fever pitch on the morning of the race. It was time for the nightmare that is team passes. The authorities issue thirty passes that give access to the circuit itself and, ultimately, to the holy of holies – the inner paddock.

Each additional pass required costs 300 Euros. The essential team personnel, including drivers, management, catering, technical, mechanics and support staff, totalled thirty-two. There were probably another 100 people with greater or lesser claims to a team pass – sponsors big and small, senior Morgan management, wives, girlfriends, general friends, well-wishers and hopefuls. Our budget for extra passes was nil. This was mathematics even I could easily do.

As each member of the core team arrived, I made them sign for their pass and left them in no doubt about the importance of not losing it or lending it to anyone, under any circumstances. I hid the remaining passes deep inside the truck and told no one where they were. With many very handy hands now on the case, the pit garage was transformed in a few hours, from a shell to a very presentable home of which we could all be proud. For me, it was great to see all the planning and thinking come together; the huge backdrops, printed with big blow-up photos of the car and the finishing touch – the 'Morgan' script in purple neon which was strung above the entrance to the garage. I had spotted this light box languishing in a corner of the factory and had asked them to load it up at the last minute. It looked great.

It was also good to see the way the whole team gelled into action immediately. They already knew each other, they and established their strengths and weaknesses and sorted out their relationships. They knew who their boss was, what was expected of them and nothing was outside their capabilities. And they were simply delighted to be there. You could see it in their faces; willing, eager, confident, enjoying every minute of it. While it was still relatively easy to get in and out of the circuit, I spent a lot of time out on shopping missions. Some things, like food and drink, were easy. Other essentials, which might range from paint, drill bits or knicker elastic, could be more difficult to track down. Every time I handed over my long-suffering credit cards, something in the back of my mind rang a warning bell. But there was no option. The stuff was needed and nobody else was going to pay.

Robert and the early part of his entourage arrived later that afternoon. Once again, he had taken on Anne Morel to work with him. Once again, I knew nothing about this prior to his arrival. I needed this clarified, so I asked him what exactly was her role. He told me that she was there to look after local French language PR for Adam and of course she was available for any translation we might need and maybe liaison with the French race authorities. I could see problems on the horizon, so I wanted to draw a line in the sand. I asked Robert to ensure that Anne knew very clearly that she should not talk to any media other than French language people and that it was very important that she did nothing in respect of team management issues without first referring to me and the others. He quickly put my mind to rest, saying that Anne would be very busy looking after Adam's schedule of PR activity.

The substance of this conversation may have satisfied my immediate concerns, but I remained very sceptical about the overall situation. There were too many agendas being pursued already and enormous potential for trouble in the political structure that was evolving. Maddy and I escaped for a quiet coffee while I tried to explain to her what was going on and why it was going to be important to keep a close eye on PR matters. As usual, Maddy was not slow to grasp the nettle.

Thankfully, there was too much to do to spend time worrying about what might happen. The first round of media interviews started as early bird journalists arrived. I was pleased to see that the concerted effort we had made over the past eighteen months had largely worked. People knew all about the trials and tribulations of Morgan Works – the ACO's rejection, the Donington fiasco, the crash at Spa, the scrutineering nightmares and the final redemptions at Bugatti and Sebring. They knew all about our lack of money too.

The British media firmly believes itself to be the most important in the world. It has a point. The science and art of publishing is probably more developed in the UK than it is anywhere else. And with English established, at least for the moment, as the only really global language for print, broadcast and internet publishing, it is not surprising that the London-based editors and journalists often feel very self-important. But at Le Mans, the Brits had to take their place on a very international stage. We were easily as popular with the French, Belgian, German, Spanish, Italian and Japanese media as we were with the British. People from everywhere know, understand and love the 'David and Goliath' story; the idea that the little guy can take on the big boys is not limited by borders, and there are versions everywhere from China to Venezuela. So the Morgan Works story had caught and fired their imaginations.

Most of the British media knew and liked our story too. Of course, there were one or two important exceptions; people who loathed everything about Morgan for whatever personal reasons and in one specific case, a motorsport 'expert' news journalist who simply could not see past the end of his nose. He was firmly of the 'only winners matter' school. Sadly for him, this put him completely out of line with the huge numbers of his British readership who were now our loyal fans.

Maddy and I were kept very busy with back-to-back pre-race interviews. There were also several major, on-going PR projects that we had started several months before – two TV documentaries that were in progress and several magazine features where we had agreed to lend journalists a Morgan road car to drive down to Le Mans. One of the big British TV companies turned up and I did a follow-up interview with them out on the pit lane. I knew the producer well by now, as we had already had arranged interviews back home with myself and with Adam Sharpe. I finished the interview and headed back to the little office in the truck, where another journalist was waiting for an interview. Minutes later Anne Morel came running through the garage, very excited about the TV crew she had pinned down outside. She was desperate to find Adam for an interview.

As soon as I had finished the press interview, I went out to see what was going on. Just as I had feared, Anne was overwhelming the film crew with enthusiasm; and it was the same crew I had previously dealt with. I had been exasperated many times before during this journey. Now I was absolutely furious. Only a few hours before I had had the conversation with Robert about vital lines of delineation – and here we were, with Anne jumping all over a sensitive British media relationship that Maddy and I had worked hard on for months, in direct contravention of what we had agreed. Worse, we had already ensured the TV people had an interview with Adam in the can. They did not want or need another, but were too polite to refuse Anne's very pushy approach. We were in great danger of appearing disorganised – and foolish.

I found Robert and made my feelings very plain. For once, he seemed to understand my point of view and promised to talk to Anne. But the cancer that had been eating away at the Morgan Works project ever since Bugatti was now perilously close to the jugular. My only allegiance – and the best part of my life for the past two years – was to the Morgan Works Team and through that vehicle, the Morgan brand and what it represented. Every ounce of professional effort and determination was focused on that target. Robert appeared to have no interest whatever in the Morgan Works Team or the Morgan brand, except inasmuch as it could provide a stepping stone for Adam's career. There was nothing wrong in that stance and the two positions were not mutually exclusive. It could, and should, have been a joint and mutually beneficial exercise. Instead, we were fighting each other.

There was little time to dwell. At times, there was a queue of people who wanted to talk; media, sponsors, members of the team. The rest of the day vaporised in a haze of quick fire discussions and decisions. There were now increasingly visible signs of the deep split within the camp. Robert and his private entourage were staying in a chateau he had rented, away from the rest of the team. A small motor home, which I had insisted we needed on site as an office and rest area for the drivers, was immediately taken over by Robert, Anne and his private staff as the HQ for their own campaign. During the entire stay on site, I never entered this motor home.

My mobile phone almost glowed from constant phone calls and text messages. Among dozens of messages, I received one from Robert. 'Injunction threatened by xxx company to impound car at scrutineering. I know I have paid MY bills. You better phone home, ET.' It is hard to explain how so much venom could be packed into a short text message.

I was grateful for years of PR crisis management training and experience. Rule one: get the facts. I called the factory and within an hour the problem – which had been caused by a commercial confusion stretching back well before my time to the 2002 campaign – was easily resolved. I doubted if the fault lines beneath the surface of the Morgan Works Team would be mended so simply, if ever.

As this was the first night that everyone was together and our on-site catering didn't start serving until the following day, we all met up in a restaurant near the team hotel for dinner. It was to be the last time we all sat down at the same table.

Scrutineering day was upon us. The team was at the circuit early and the car was polished until it gleamed. When the time came, a transporter arrived to take the car down to the city centre park, where the fun and games would take place.

Just as we prepared for the final and most important scrutineering session of the whole campaign, I learned of another threatened injunction that could very publicly kill our dream. This time, it did not concern Morgan or me in any way. I passed on the message to Robert, with my faith in Karma revitalised. It was his turn to address a misunderstanding from the past.

Robert, Anne and the drivers travelled to town in his car. They left early. David Bradley, Mark Baldwin, Rogier Vancamelbecke and I were to follow in my car. Finally we were ready in clean team clothes, paperwork and camera all prepared. We jumped into the Volvo, which I had managed to get right into the paddock enclosure. I fired up the engine. There was a big cloud of steam from beneath the bonnet. It did not look good. Time was running out.

I felt a tinge of panic in my guts as we quickly decided to abandon the stricken car. If we were late for signing on, we would be in big trouble. We raced across to where our catering team was unloading. Begging on our knees, we persuaded them to give us a lift down town. Bradders and Mark clambered in the back of the van, among trays of food and drinks. As we were battling through heavy traffic, I received a terse text message from Robert. 'It is MANDATORY that you are here as team manager.' My reply was equally short. 'I know that. En route.'

The absence of trust was now total and open. Later, Robert admitted that he had overheard a conversation I had been having that morning, when he heard me say 'No, I'm not going…' I had been talking about the Driver's Parade taking

The car enters the Le Mans scrutineering tents for the final and most important checks of all. (David Dowse)

For the first time ever, the Morgan Works Team Aero 8 achieves a 100 per cent score in scrutineering. (Melissa Warren)

place later, but Robert had jumped to the conclusion that I couldn't be bothered to attend the vital official administrative session. A very French farce. We had a completely clean bill of health from the scrutineers. As usual, they went through the whole elaborate ritual, measuring everything, meticulously ticking every box on the endless forms. At the end of it all, we looked in amazement at our 100 per cent score. It was the first time that we had ever achieved a full house. 'That ought to be framed for the workshop wall,' Bradders commented dryly.

More French farce followed, as the team, drivers and the car lined up for the huge bank of photographers. Maddy and I, who between us had handled hundreds of photo shoots, began organising the line up. Then Anne Morel appeared and started re-organising things and shouting in French to the largely British photographers who were up on a high scaffolding overlooking the scene. Finally, Robert added his own input, trying to ensure that Adam stood out from the crowd. The whole thing was a chaotic, amateurish mess. I looked across at Maddy, whose face showed both her professional insight into what was happening and at the same time genuine sympathy for my impossible predicament.

'Come on, let's go and find a cold beer,' I said to her.

Despite the bullshit, another two boxes on my long list of project goals were now firmly ticked. The car was cleared for racing. All three drivers were successfully signed on for practice and qualifying. There were only three boxes

Good reason to smile. From left to right; David Dowse, Wim Wenders, Rogier Vancamelbecke, Mark Baldwin, David Bradley, Neil Cunningham, Adam Sharpe and Steve Hyde pose for the cameras following the team's most successful scrutineering ever. (DailySportsCar.com)

left; get the drivers qualified; start the race; finish the race. It was time for some action on the track.

9.7 - Minimum qualifying time:
Drivers shall achieve a lap time at least equal to 125% of the average of
the 3 best laps set by 3 cars of different makes and at least equal to 115% of the best time achieved by the fastest car in each of the four categories.

Let's remind ourselves. Just a few short weeks had passed since the dramatic test weekend, when the hapless Keith Ahlers had had his disagreement with the concrete wall. In that time, a huge amount of work had been done on the car to repair the crash damage, sort out the other issues and complete the deep maintenance needed to prepare for the 24 Hours. With that in mind, for the car to have passed the toughest scrutineering in the world with flying colours was a superb achievement.

But the cold facts were that the car had not turned a wheel since the final lap at the test weekend. There had simply been no time even for a shakedown test before we left to travel to France. So as the lights went green at 1900 for the opening of the first qualifying session on Wednesday evening, we were back in unknown territory.

Above: Slow progress: early qualifying sessions were well off pace. (Melissa Warren)

Below: Steve Hyde passes on vital track conditions to Neil Cunningham as the battle for qualifying continues. (DailySportsCar.com)

As Top Gun, Neil took on the first few shakedown laps. The car seemed fine and all three drivers put in several familiarisation laps. Then we started to try for some times. The car was slow – slower than we had been at the test weekend, although nothing of any significance had been changed. I put it down to nerves. We needed a little time to settle down. The times improved, but not enough. The first session ended at 2100 and there was an hour break before the night session began.

Bradders and Mark Baldwin huddled over the data along with Ian Beveridge, Yokohama's tyre specialist, trying to see where things could be improved. There was no point in interfering in the technical discussion. I went to the office in the truck, read over the rules again and crunched some numbers on a calculator. We needed a steep improvement if we were to be safely inside the qualifying envelope. Outside, I caught sight of Robert, standing away from the camp, deep in thought and with a look of pure malice on his face. The second session did not go much better. All three drivers improved, but they were still several seconds off what was needed. The camp was very glum as the session ended at midnight. The technical team and the drivers huddled into the tiny motorhome for a debrief. Again I stayed away, waiting close by in case they reached a decision that needed some action from me.

Robert walked up to me in the dark. 'Are you OK, Robert? I asked calmly.

'Only just.' He said, his voice full of choked anger.

'The guys are in there now, working it out,' I said.

'Yes, but who's directing them, David?' He almost spat the words, then walked away. I saw him a few minutes later in the distance, talking animatedly into his mobile phone.

The meeting went on for a long time. Robert came back and I watched him push his way into the already cramped, tiny room. Whatever course their discussion was taking, I was quite sure that intervention from either Robert or myself was unlikely to be constructive at this point.

This is a matter of management style. I knew that nobody needed to impress upon Dave Bradley and Mark Baldwin the vital importance of finding some answers. They would be feeling the weight on their shoulders quite as intensely as it was possible to feel any responsibility. This is a natural outcome of empowerment as a policy. For this reason, I was sure that only someone with a very high degree of technical knowledge, specific to the Aero 8, should intervene in the technical discussion. Delegation demands real trust – on both sides. I also knew that if they needed anything, they would ask me and I believed they would then trust me to deliver it.

I have never seen Bradders, Mark and Rogier so depressed as they were on the minibus when we finally left the circuit around two that morning. Nobody spoke. Nobody wanted to stop for a beer. It was as if the life force had been sucked out of them.

Early the following morning, I received a text message from Robert informing me that Darrell was on his way from Australia and should be with us by the evening. I shared this news with the others over breakfast. 'So we can all relax then, gentlemen,' I suggested bleakly.

Bradders and Mark spent a long time on the phone that day. Opinions and ideas were sought from Christopher Lawrence, the factory, engine specialists Mader, Lutz Passon, our KW Suspension man, Mick Boasman at Magnetti Marelli and others. They worked quietly and methodically, without apparent stress. Adjustments were made to suspension settings and the rear spoiler. There was no sign of Robert all day. Maddy and I were busy with more media activity. Several foreign journalists came by, expressing genuine concern for our qualifying times and wishing us the very best of luck for the next session. In stark contrast, one of our 'loyal' British media friends opened with the helpful question, 'Doesn't look like you're going to make it, does it?' We did not offer him a coffee.

Our sponsors from racinglines.com arrived to install the equipment for the web cam and Matthew Parkin got to work preparing for the first live web cast. I prayed there would be good news for us to tell people when we went live. The day passed in a flash and before we knew it, it was time for the next, crucial qualifying session. Robert appeared and sat to one side, speaking to no one. There was no sign of Darrell and no further mention of him. Nor was there any time to worry about him.

The track lights went green. Neil roared off. He did one settling lap after his out lap, then went for his first flyer. We were all glued to the timing screen.

We heard Neil roar past on the pit straight. It was a quite unmistakable sound. There followed a few seconds of eternity before the time appeared. 4.24! Neil had blasted 6 seconds off the previous night's best and placed himself well inside the qualifying window.

He was soon back in for the change to Adam, who immediately booked his own place in the race with a lap of 4.26. Steve Hyde followed shortly afterwards with a 4.28. All three drivers had qualified safely. The crowd, especially the large numbers of Morgan fans who had colonised the grandstand opposite our pit garage, cheered, waved their flags and blasted their horns. A couple of fireworks went off in celebration. The atmosphere in the camp changed incredibly – from the deepest stress and anxiety to sheer elation and exquisite relief. The rollercoaster ride continued. Now it really felt like we were back at Le Mans.

During the break, the team changed the differential; part of the planned engineering schedule. Neil took it out when the track opened again, put in four laps to bed the new components in and then came home. Within 20 minutes, the garage was packed away and the doors closed. Bradders and Mark Baldwin were beaming like reprieved men. 'Beer o'clock, I reckon,' said Bradders. Back at the circuit the next morning, our first journalist visitor wanted to know what had gone wrong.

'Sorry, I don't understand the question,' I said honestly.

Apparently, Radio Le Mans had reported that there must be problems in the Morgan camp, as they had shut up their garage so early the night before.

Neil Cunningham finally books a place on the start line for the Le Mans 2004 race. (DailySportsCar.com)

'Oh, no, we didn't have a problem at all. We got everyone safely qualified, bedded in a new diff, then we went to the pub.' I said. 'That's the Morgan way.'

Over breakfast at the hotel, I had asked Bradders and Mark Baldwin what it was they had done to make the car go quicker. All I got in reply were shrugged shoulders. 'Not much, really.' Either they were keeping something to themselves, or there was another factor in play here – maybe the drivers had simply pulled their fingers out, believing that the car had been improved. Either scenario is entirely possible. There is no track activity on Friday at Le Mans. The day before race day is devoted to huge crowds, photographers, media and the razzmatazz of the Driver's Parade in the evening. Robert had also arranged a barbeque at the chateau for guests, sponsors and the team. True to form, the Morgan Works Team decided to use this relatively restful day to change the engine. Otherwise, they claimed, they may have got bored.

During the morning Darrell finally arrived after his long haul from Australia. He received a warm welcome from the team members who had met him in Florida, but with the complex engine change in full swing, there was little for him to do except sit around keeping an eye on things for his boss. It was with a

Morgan at Le Mans

Above: Dreams – who knows what these kids were thinking as they watched the Morgan Works Team burning the midnight oil? (David Dowse)

Opposite above: Darrell Dixon keeps watch as the Morgan Team gets on with the Friday night engine change. (David Dowse)

Opposite below: Hard graft – the team pushes on with the engine change. (David Dowse)

wry smile that I reflected how much Robert's lack of faith in the Morgan Team had cost him. He had flown Darrell all the way from Sydney to ensure Adam qualified for the big race; qualifying was already history. The subject was never mentioned again.

Just as in 2002, we were busy all day with huge crowds of well-wishers. And just as in 2002, by the end of the afternoon Maddy and I were both hoarse from talking. We did our best to keep people away from the team working on the engine change inside the garage. British TV News came along to do an interview and we set them up with Bradders and Mark Baldwin; it was their show, really.

Adrian Clements	John Emberson	Andrew Brookes	Giampiero Pecelli	John W Schutz	Peter Ives Ruland
Alberto Olivieri	Kees Kruit	Andrew Graves	Gordon Criag	Kevin Cheale	Peter M MacIntyre
Andrew Brookes	Klaus Rehm	Angus Matheson	Greg Miller	L Sebba	Philippe Georgen
Andrew Graves	Knut Hallan	Axel Schwarz	Gregory Powick	Lawrence Krueger	Roger Iain Tatton
Andy Low	Laurence Summerhill	Bart Hamilton the 2nd	Henry Dowse	Lisa Salazar	Stephen D Balsamo
Bjorn Schage	Morgan Sports Car Club	Bart Hamilton the 3rd	Ian S Matthews	M E A Ireland	Teri Hamilton
Brian Ward	Nicholas Morgan	Brian Ward	Jack Payne	Michael Hattam	Teri Hyde
Brynjar Skauvik	Peter Burrows	David Waite	James D Barry	Michael J Swedler	Thomas F Faught Jnr
Carlo Hasenoehrl	Peter Scott	David Waite	James Graves	Michael Virr	Thomas Finger
Dennis McClellan	Richard Fohl	Eloise Hedbor	James Nicol	Morgan Sports Car Club	Tim FitzGerald
Eduardo Sanchez	Richard Thorne	Eric Bardsley	James W Fisher	Nicholas Cavitt	Vernon Dale Johnson
Ilya Gryanik	Robert Stones	Gary L Kneislay	John Bradford	Paul Cardy	William Hughes
James Graves	Simon Skelding	George Edwards	John D Brownlie	Paul Roblett	
James Tebby	Stephen D Balsamo				
Joep Westerveld	Ver Ecke Dominiek				
John Bradford					

With the entire Sharpe camp away getting ready for the Drivers' Parade and the evening barbeque, we set about organising ourselves for the long battle ahead. Water was stockpiled everywhere – under the truck, around the garage; anywhere space could be found. A final shopping trip was organised. This would be the last chance of getting anything in to the paddock. The shopping list included a first-aid kit, a selection of batteries, large amounts of chewing gum and sweets, bin bags, mosquito repellent, sun cream, paracetemol and toilet paper. Team race uniforms went to be cleaned. During the afternoon, VIP guests began to arrive; Morgan chairman Alan Garnett; members of the Morgan family; Eric Sturzda from Banque Barings Brothers; senior executives from Yokohama, Japan. I juggled the precious passes in a desperate attempt to accommodate everyone.

Relative calm descended in the early evening as most people went off to town for the spectacular parade. I offered time off to those mechanics who were not directly involved in the engine change. There were very few takers; they preferred to stay with the car and their team-mates until it was finished. Those who weren't wielding a spanner polished and re-polished the body panels and prepared spare parts that everybody hoped would never be needed. I had never seen morale better. The evening wore on. It was time for the barbeque. 'Does anyone want to go?' I asked. Again, there were no takers. There was still plenty of work to be done.

As midnight approached, the engine fired up. Diagnostic checks were run. The garage was tidied and swept clean. All was as ready as it was ever going to be. Our favourite bar was still open as we drove past. The first cold beer was downed in quiet reverence. Only one more was permissible the night before race day. No rules were mentioned. It wasn't even necessary for me to call time; as the bottles were emptied, everyone filed out to the minibus without a murmur of protest.

Opposite above: Crowds jostle for a view of one of the most popular cars in the Le Mans 2004 pit lane. (David Dowse)

Opposite below: Over eighty individuals supported the Morgan Works Team's crusade. Their names were carried on the boot lid of the car. (David Dowse)

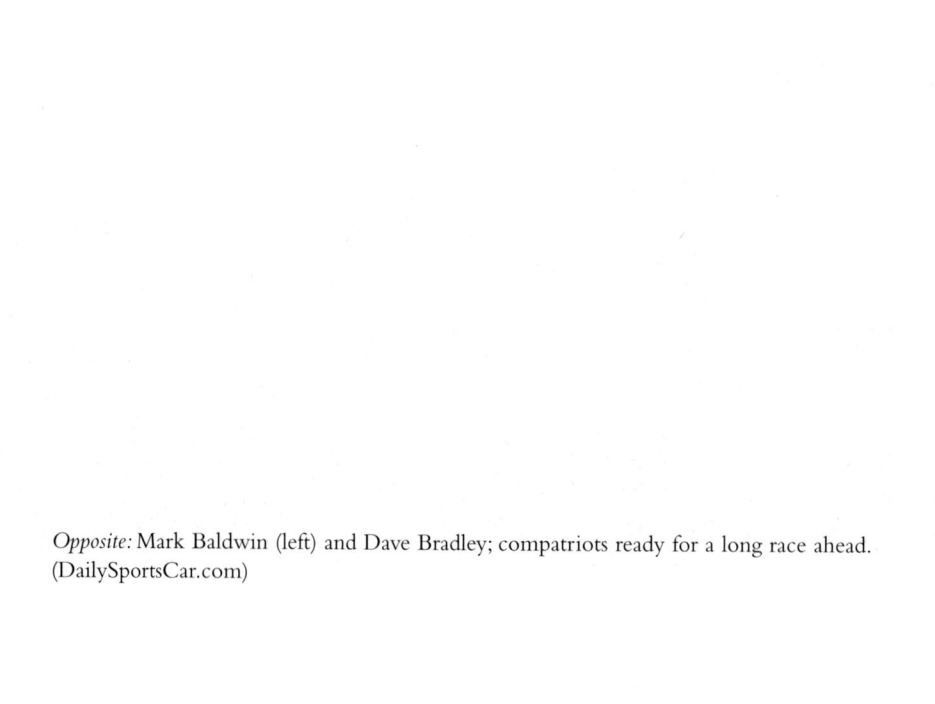

Opposite: Mark Baldwin (left) and Dave Bradley; compatriots ready for a long race ahead. (DailySportsCar.com)

seventeen

The last mile

My memory of the morning of race day is a blur of visitors arriving, juggling passes, media interviews, checking and re-checking the rules and the start schedule and wondering what had gone wrong with my relationship with Dave Bradley and Mark Baldwin.

From the earliest days, we had been close compatriots travelling together on this mad odyssey. Now, even as we prepared for the final, climatic episode, a strange coolness had crept in. I couldn't put my finger on it, but I was sure something had changed. I had my suspicions about the ultimate source of the unease, but this was not the time to ponder. We shared our toilet with the Audi Team next door. To access it, we had to make our way through the complex of buildings and tents behind their garage. On the toilet wall, I spotted a very neat, printed race day schedule for Audi that detailed in military precision the planned events of the day, from reveille at 0600 to the winner's podium and the post race celebrations. Before long, most of the Morgan Team had been in for a comfort break and to read the impressive Audi tome. When I visited again later, a handwritten sheet had been taped to the wall alongside the Audi schedule. It was the Morgan Works Race Day Schedule.

A masterful pastiche of the Audi schedule, it began:

0930 ish... bacon and eggs, read the paper
11.30 ish...wander down to pit garage, polish car again.

Sadly, this historic document did not survive the mêlée of the race.

The build up to the race start was dramatic, every bit as exciting as it had been in 2002, despite the notable lack of the flypast from the French Air Force. If anything, there seemed to be even more Brits crowding the huge grandstands. They chanted and cheered us as we waited on the grid for the start sequence to get under way. A wave of emotion welled up from deep within me. All the pain and anguish, all the stress and the mental exhaustion of the past two years flashed before me as I waved back to the crowd. God knows how, but we were here and there were just 24 hours separating us from the conclusion of our odyssey.

The whistles blew. The grid was cleared. The lights went green for the form-up lap. A strange quiet descended as the last of the cars disappeared around the first turn. All heads turned toward the other end of the pit straight. The distant rumble turned to a screaming roar and then there was the unforgettable sight and sound of a Le Mans start as the cars blasted into the first racing lap. John Burbidge and Mark Baldwin entertained the crowd opposite and the TV and web cameras by playing a card game, squatting on the floor in the front of the garage and using one of the safety stands as an impromptu table. It was this special kind of humour and spontaneity that made Morgan Works what is was and of course, people loved it.

The first 6 hours went without a single hitch. As the heat of the day faded into the cooler evening air, the times steadily improved until we were circulating around a very acceptable 4.23 and we had already moved up the field a couple of places. Stops were made only for scheduled fuel, tyre and driver changes. The temperature data was all looking good. Dave Bradley added his own piece of

The last mile

John Burbidge and Mark Baldwin entertain the cameras and the crowd with a card game in the pit garage, while a bemused official looks on. (David Dowse)

pantomime to the show, using a huge inflatable hand, decorated with an England flag, as a prop instead of the usual 'stop' board used by the front of car managers. When the car was released back to the circuit, he would use the hand to point dramatically, as though the driver might be unsure about which direction to go. Then he would use it to wave at the fans in the grandstand opposite, who would respond with a mass waving of Union Jacks. The Morgan Works Team was in its element.

Sitting in the sauna that was the office in the truck, I worked with Matthew Parkin and Maddy, preparing race press releases and feeding information to Matthew for the live web cast, which was now up and running. I had one ear of my headset on to keep in touch with the driver talkback and team instructions. The atmosphere was relaxed and happy.

What I heard over the radio from Neil a minute or so after 2200 made my blood run cold.

'I'm out of gas! I've run out of fucking gas!'

Bedlam in the camp. What the hell was going on? This should not have been possible. He was due in for fuel in another two laps and I knew that Dave Bradley had accurate fuel data and always left a margin of error. We needed facts. Where was he? What were the symptoms just before the car stopped? The radio had gone dead. We could not reach Neil. We were completely in the dark.

Above: Dave Bradley wields the famous 'hand' during one of many pit stops. (David Dowse)

Opposite: The first 6 hours pass without a hitch. (DailySportsCar.com)

Robert appeared and without any discussion took over all communications with Neil, who eventually remembered the emergency mobile phone that was kept in the cockpit. The team started working through a logical process of checks, trying to pin down what the problem was. Dave Bradley checked his numbers again. 'He should definitely have enough for another two laps. Definitely,' he said. He looked worried.

We all looked worried. The Le Mans rules in this respect are simple and unequivocal; if a car stops on the circuit, the driver must restart it on his own, using only whatever tools and equipment he has with him and without any help from anyone. If any person approaches the car within 20m, the car is immediately disqualified. The team is only permitted to give instructions. I read the rules again and again and tried to make sure that Robert understood them. By now the fuel pump was suspected and they were talking Neil through checking the various connections and pipe work. I could imagine him, out there in the dark, with cars screaming by just a few metres away, his head buried in the boot of the Aero 8, fiddling among the complex technology.

Nothing was working. Two of the team got ready to try to locate him, taking the quad bike to try to work through the heaving crowds. It would take them at

Anxious faces as the team waits desperately for news from the stricken car. (David Dowse)

least half an hour to get to him. What they would do when they got there wasn't clear, apart from shouting instructions and giving moral support. We desperately looked for any way we could get some fuel to him, if that did indeed turn out to be the problem. There was no way within the rules to do so.

An hour passed before we knew it. The life force of our dream was ebbing away. No one thought for a second about giving up, but as each extra minute went by, I began to prepare myself mentally for failure. It was so unfair. I walked away from the camp and sat alone in the dark, praying with all my heart for a miracle. Back in the camp, other technical theories had appeared and were being tested. The quad team had found Neil, but there was nothing they could do. I know they would have physically pushed the car the eight miles or so back to the pits if they were given the chance, but the marshalls were in close attendance in case anyone was tempted to breech the rules.

Midnight passed. Now another factor had come into play. In order for the result to be classified, the rules require a car to complete a percentage of the distance covered by the leading car in the race. The numbers were stacked against us, even if we did get going again. Desperate ideas were discussed and discarded, one by one. We had reached the end of the long, long road.

I was standing next to Robert, who was deep in conversation with Neil on his headset. I had taken mine off by now. Suddenly, Robert's face lit up with a smile that I had never seen on his face before. 'He's got it going! He's bloody well

The look on the faces of Dave Bradley and Mark Baldwin says it all as news comes in that Neil has got the car going again. (David Dowse)

got it going!' He was dancing around the pit garage. The whole place erupted in unabandoned joy; the crew, the sponsors, even the pit marshalls were cheering and hugging each other. Minutes later, the car was back in and the team worked furiously to replace the fuel pump. TV cameras appeared from everywhere. The crowd opposite were going nuts. At 0046, the car was back out, running smoothly with Adam at the wheel. The calculator quickly told me that there was no hope now of finishing in a classified position, but it just didn't matter any more. As one, we all knew that all we had to do was to keep the car going and finally finish our business with this impossible rollercoaster.

I grabbed Nail and took him away from the crowd that had gathered around him. 'You bastard!' I said to my friend. 'You nearly finished me off. Don't you *ever* do that again!' He told me how, after everything he tried had failed, he kicked and cursed the car, got back in the driving seat and for some reason just tried the green button one more time. The engine fired immediately and he just drove back to the pits as normal.

Left: Time for a quiet word; team manager David Dowse and lead driver Neil Cunningham. (Melissa Warren)

Opposite: Waiting. With the car out and running well, there's often not much happening in the pits. (David Dowse)

Later, there were many theories about what had happened out there at Arnage. The most plausible one is that the car actually did run out of fuel. Neil had been putting in some very fast laps just before it happened and maybe this, combined with track and atmospheric conditions, increased fuel consumption enough to throw Dave Bradley's figures out. What then happened may have been that as the car stood for a while, the residual bubbled fuel in the pipelines all eventually settled back into the fuel pump, producing enough to fire it up and get Neil back to the pits.

Or it might have been a loose electrical connection.

Certainly the team took no chances when the car did come in; they replaced the whole fuel pump assembly in just a few minutes.

After the incredible drama of those 2 unforgettable hours, things settled down as the night progressed into the small hours. It's a surreal time. After most of the crowd has finally faded away to their tents and hotels, the teams along the pit lane are isolated on an island of bright lights. The night is rent every couple of minutes by the roar of a race car blasting down the pit straight, the

Mark Baldwin grabs vital sleep between pit stops. (David Dowse)

disappearing into the dark around the turn, its brakes glowing bright red for a brief moment. For the crew, there's little to do but wait for the next scheduled stop, keep warm, nap and eat. It was during these few hours that the festering sore that had been the catering issue ever since the Bugatti race months before finally broke. The team would put up with every hardship imaginable, so long as they were well fed and watered. This was why we had fought so hard to have the service we wanted. Now, in the dead of the night, when it was needed most, the food wasn't coming often enough, it wasn't good enough and it wasn't hot enough. I spoke to the caterers several times, but things did not improve. Robert disappeared, returning with a pile of sausage and chips he had bought from one of the public cafés. He had that look on his face again. I had no doubt that trouble would follow.

Dawn. In an exact repeat of 2002, I drove out to the Porsche Curves with Matthew Parkin to watch the car go past a few times as the sun came up. It was the same moving, dramatic experience that it had been then, but different in one important respect – this was our car, our team, our Le Mans race. It was there, standing ankle deep in empty beer cans and the other remains of the night's parties, that I began to realise what we had achieved.

Then I recalled how far we had got in 2002, only to be disappointed. It was by now 0600. There were still 10 hours of racing to go. At 0630, the car came in with a broken throttle cable. Once again, the fates were with us. – Had the cable broken anywhere on the circuit other than where it did – just as the car approached the pit lane – it would have been fatal. It took a while to fix, but eventually, the car went back out. 'Well, that woke us up,' said Bradders. 'Any chance of a coffee?'

For the next few hours, the only drama came from one of the crew piling several spoons of salt into his coffee instead of sugar. I sat for a long time with my feet in a bucket of cold water. The blisters on the soles of my feet, caused by long hours of standing and walking in the searing heat, had broken and the flesh was completely raw. Every step I took now was excruciating. Wim, a Belgian friend of Rogier's who had joined the team as a volunteer tyre washer, silently offered me a brand new pair of socks. It was one of the kindest and most welcome gestures I have ever received from anyone.

At 0930 the car came in with a broken radiator. It is at this stage, after more than 17 hours of racing, that the endurance team has to search deep down in its

Nothing compares to sunrise at Le Mans, with the car still running well…
(DailySportsCar.com)

reserve tanks. This is when things are most likely to start going wrong with the car and it is also when the team is likely to be most tired. The bigger teams, like our friends at Audi next door, can afford to bring out fresh people from their soundproofed, air-conditioned sleeping pods to begin a new shift. Not Morgan Works. The same people who had run the car all night were now working flat out, against the clock, to replace the radiator.

I caught Dave Bradley looking long and hard at engine data while the others worked. 'What is it, Dave?' 'Oil,' he said quietly. 'She's using a lot of oil.' 'Is there anything we can do?' 'Nope. Just keep filling the thing up.' I may not have been especially technical, but I knew quite enough to realise that engine oil leaks were usually the precursor of failure. It was just a matter of time. As the morning wore on, we passed the point at which the engine had failed in 2002. Nobody dared to mention this particular milestone. And this time, I could not allow myself to think about finishing. I did not want to tempt fate.

Bradders was looking intently now at the data after every scheduled pit stop. The water temperatures were high and rising and the oil leak was getting worse. The stage was set for an engine failure. We told the drivers to ease off a little to reduce stress on the engine. It simply didn't matter how fast we went now; we just had to nurse her home.

Midday passed, just 4 hours to go. The car was needing oil and water at every scheduled stop now. Bradders had stopped looking at his data. 'It just makes me worry more,' he explained. At around 1330 another radiator blew, this time punctured by a stone thrown up on the track by another car. It had gone through the radiator like an armour piercing bullet. As the bonnet panel were lifted off, a huge cloud, a mixture of steam and smoke from the oil leak, filled the whole garage. The team did a fantastic job, changing the radiator in record time and sending the car back out. There were just two hours left to run.

A delegation from the race authorities visited the garage and asked to speak with me. Usually, this meant trouble. Had we infringed some rule? With the exhaustion and stress about whether the car was going to make it and the deafening noise from the track, it took me a little while to understand what they were telling me. When it did finally sink in, it was the most incredible news. We had been chosen by a committee of the great and good to receive a special award – given to the best technical crew in the race. We were asked to provide the names of four individuals and the officials said they would return, with champagne and trophies, just before the race finished.

Choosing the names was something of a problem. Each and every one of them deserved recognition. But choose we had to and in the end there was only one outcome possible. David Bradley, Mark Baldwin and Rogier Vancamelbecke were the key people who had kept the car going, not just for this race, but all through the long, hard road that had lead us here. John Burbidge, though he had only recently returned to the fold, had been there in 2002 and had done a faultless job this time, too. He had earned his trophy.

The news flew around the garage and suddenly everyone was smiling. I felt deeply emotional and had to go off on my own for a while. After all the anguish, all the fighting and all the trouble, this was the most wonderful news I could possibly imagine. The fact that it was the team that had been recognised was pure poetry. It was as if the whole desperate effort was finally vindicated and rewarded. And, just as I had been telling anyone who would listen since the very beginning, it wasn't about the car, it wasn't about the drivers, it wasn't about how fast we could go and it certainly wasn't about winning the race. No. It was about the people. The incredible, unique and special people whose grit, determination, humour in the face of adversity and sheer will-power made everything possible. It was this humanity that I had seen here in 2002. It was this spirit that had sparked off the whole crazy, impossible journey.

But the fat lady had not sung yet… The next scheduled stop was upon us and a lot more oil and water were needed. She was hanging on by a thread. With a new and mighty spring in their steps, the crew conducted the whole pit stop with a consummate artistry that is impossible to describe. Everyone began to pray. There was one more scheduled stop to go.

The minutes ticked away. The Aero 8 kept going round. As the final pit stop approached, the garage started filling up with more and more people, desperate to be close to the action; to be a part of it.

The car came in. Smoke and steam billowed from all around the bonnet. She was on her very last legs. To be absolutely safe, they put the trolley under the car, swung it through ninety degrees and backed it into the garage. More oil, more water and many prayers were applied. They pushed her out again on the trolley. Then, before they sent her out for the final stint, Bradders signed with his huge hand, round and round. 'Swing her right round, boys!' he said over the crew radios. Slowly and sedately, the car was paraded for the camera and the crowd in a full 360 circle. She came to a stop, pointing the right way up the pit lane.

They dropped the air jacks smartly. The engine fired. Bradders waved his hand. 'Go!'

Huge cheers erupted from the crowded garage and we could clearly hear the cheers echoing around the grandstand opposite. The excitement and the crowd in the garage carried on building. There was now only just over an hour to go. The French authorities arrived, with magnums of champagne and huge gleaming trophies for the four mechanics who were accepting the honour on behalf of all their team mates. The award cited the superb presentation of the car at scrutineering, the presentation of the pit garage, the presentation of the team themselves and their superb work during the race itself. It was a complete testament to everything that made Morgan Works what is was. Cameras flashed. Everyone was shaking hands. Many were hugging each other. But the race had not finished yet.

Morgan at Le Mans

The best team in the world celebrates its official recognition – as the Best Team in the World. (David Dowse)

CHAMBRE DE COMMERCE DU MANS
24 HEURES 2004
PRIX ESCRA
"MEILLEURE ASSISTANCE TECHNIQUE"

The coveted ESCRA award. (David Dowse)

We were on the last few laps. The pressure of people in the garage was so great that it was becoming difficult to stay within the mandatory line at the front – any unauthorised crossing of this line could bring us a big fine. I had heard during the team managers' briefing that the teams were strictly forbidden from running across to the pit wall at the end of the race, but I could see no way anyone was going to enforce this ruling. I didn't even bother trying.

The car blasted by – now the final lap was under way. She was going to make it! My heart almost stopped as every atom of my being prayed that nothing would happen in the final 4 minutes. There was an enormous, impossible surge as everyone rushed across the pit lane to the wall. A hapless marshall tried desperately to repel the crowd, but he didn't have a hope. I looked down the pit lane. All the other teams were assailing the wall too, like a charge in a medieval battle. The marshalls simply gave up. We all jostled for a view.

Morgan at Le Mans

The race leaders screamed by, the chequered flag waving them to victory. The other cars followed; each one representing a personal victory for another team, each with a whole story of their own behind them. And then, right at the end, around the final bend came the Morgan. The crowd on the grandstands went wild. Fireworks and flares exploded. Adam Sharpe, who had the honour of driving the final session, put on a final spurt of speed down the pit straight. The chequered flag waved. The odyssey was over.

Above: A moment of history; the Morgan Aero 8 crosses the finishing line at les 24 Heures Du Mans, 2004. (DailySportsCar.com)

Opposite: The teams jostle for position on the pit wall as the car comes into sight for the final time. (DailySportsCar.com)

Morgan at Le Mans

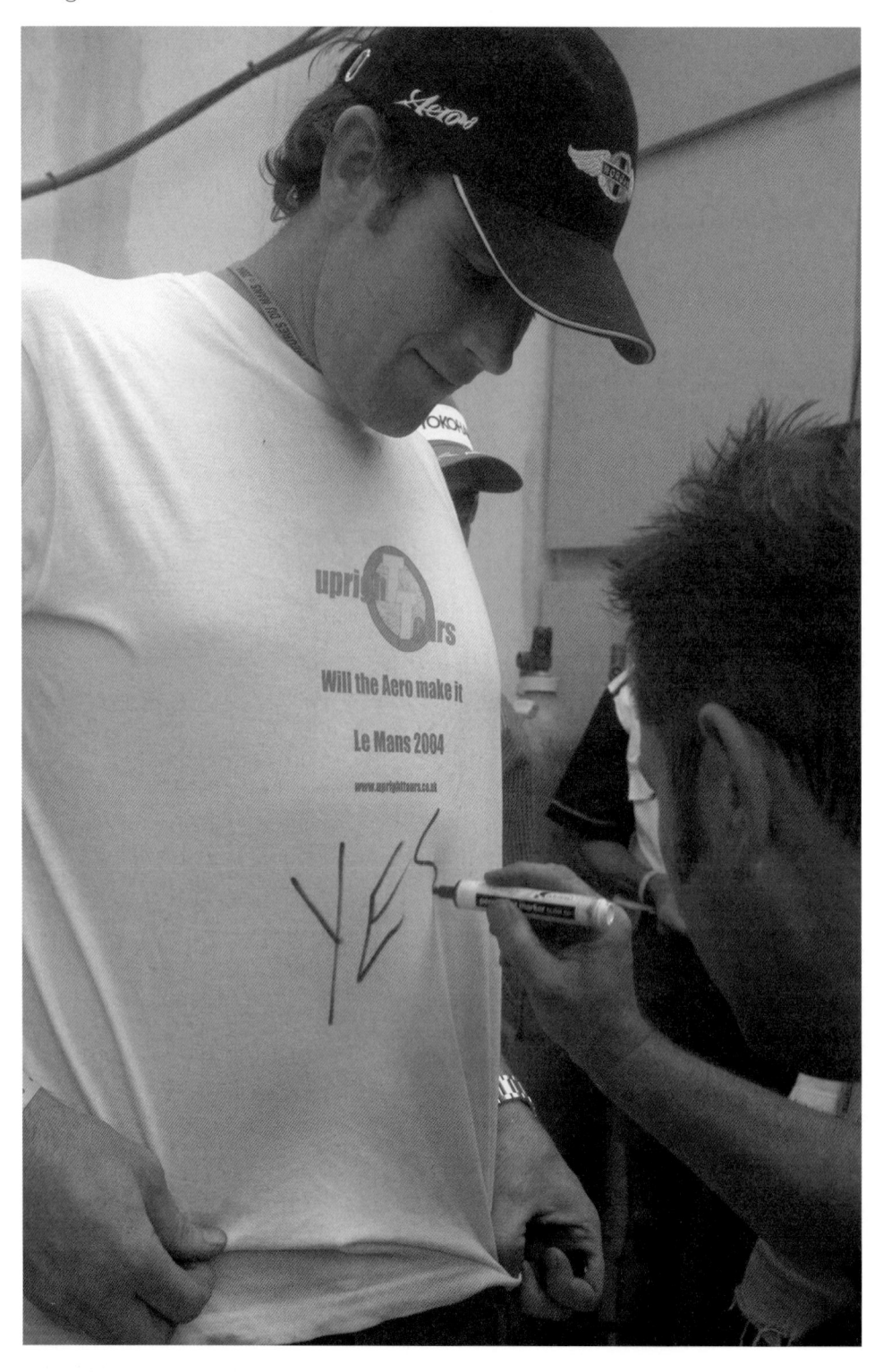

David Bradley answers a big question! (DailySportsCar.com)

Epilogue

For the first time in forty-two years, a hand-built, wooden-framed Morgan sports car had crossed the line at the Le Mans 24 Hour race. We had done it with very minimum funding. Armed only with a belief in ourselves, we had overcome political wrangling and technical failures.

But I believe the most important thing we did was to show that anyone, no matter how humble, can do anything they set out to do if only they have the right motivation, enough faith and big, open hearts. Then the passion, the spirit that lies deep within us all, can shine out and touch people in a truly meaningful way. To give joy, to *really* communicate, to break down the barriers of ego, greed and malice; these are surely among the highest aspirations we can have. The vehicle that helps us do so may be an Aero 8, a wheelchair or simply our own two feet. It's the spirit that matters.

Whatever I personally did, I believe it was done without macho posturing and without bullying – but instead, with genuine respect for the team, the car, the people who built it and those who had gone before.

Immediately after the race, I took a desperately needed holiday in Crete with my family. My watch, which had done such constant active service during the past two years, stopped working the moment our aeroplane landed. I have not worn a watch since that moment.

The long hours, weekend working and constant travelling had taken a tremendous toll on my relationship with my wife. The deep concerns about the financial situation proved well founded and as I feared I was left with serious debts from the huge expenses bills that I was unable to recover from anywhere. To add further injury, I had not been paid for any of my time on the Le Mans project since the Spa race in August 2003 and my PR business turned out to have been mortally wounded by the inordinate amount of time that the Le Mans campaign had sucked up.

As part of a wide-ranging cost-cutting programme, Morgan Motor Company ended its PR contract with Transmission PR shortly after the race. I believe that what we did will prove in the long run to have been of substantial benefit to Morgan's business, though in this respect it is quite possible that the 2004 Le

Mans race will never be given the full credit it is due. It is a great pity that there was no concerted attempt to maximise the benefits. No one can deny that we have added to the legend.

Others will have taken what they variously wanted from the journey – be it wages, career development, ego massage, professional recognition or perhaps a particularly cheap outing to the world's most prestigious race. Some people were undoubtedly damaged along the way and to them I apologise sincerely; things were not always under the control I would have wished. The deep fault lines that appeared towards the end of the journey eventually split everything asunder. But Morgan Works had done its work.

It has been a big price to pay. But for my part, I can regret nothing of what has happened to me. I have learned a great deal and experienced something great that I feel extremely proud to say I played a part in. But once is definitely, absolutely, categorically, enough.

Never again!

The Morgan Works Le Mans 2004 Team

David Dowse – Team Manager
Robert Sharpe – Commercial Manager
David Bradley – Technical Manager
Mark Baldwin – Chief Mechanic
Rogier Vancamelbecke – Race Mechanic
John Burbidge – Race Mechanic
Richard Prosser – Morgan Mechanic
Dave Groves – Morgan Mechanic
Mark Middleton – Morgan Mechanic
Ian Weaver – Morgan Mechanic
Wayne Duggan – Morgan Mechanic
Mark Davies – Pit logistics
Lutz Passon – KW Suspension
Mick Boasman – Data systems
Ian Beveridge – Yokohama
Wim Wenders – Tyre man
Bradley Marney – Goffer
Maddy Phelps – PR
Matthew Parkin – Webcast
David Morgan – Web support
Fanny Blossier – Accommodation
Darrell Dixon – Himself

Absent friends:
Christopher and Carey Lawrence
Steve Lawrence
Steve Morris
Natasha Waddington
Ben Coles
Tim FitzGerald

If you are interested in purchasing other books published by Tempus,
or in case you have difficulty finding any Tempus books in your local bookshop,
you can also place orders directly through our website

www.tempus-publishing.com